Also by KAREN GILDEN

Tea & Bee's Milk: Our Year in a Turkish Village
    —with Ray Gilden
How to Plan Your Trip to Europe
    —with Ray Gilden

CAMPING WITH THE COMMUNISTS

Camping
with the
Communists

The Adventures of an American
Family in the Soviet Union

Karen Gilden

Artha Press, Sisters, Oregon 2013

ISBN 978-1-886922-00-6
E-book ISBN 978-1-886922-01-3
Library of Congress Control Number: 2013919364

Photographs by Ray Gilden, © 1977, 2013
Trip map by Joanne McLennan, © 2013
Printed in the United States of America

Artha Press
Sisters, Oregon 97759

For Melina

CONTENTS

PREFACE

I DON'T KNOW why I waited so long to write this. Thirty-six years is plenty of time to mull something over. Still, some things need mulling, and I don't mind admitting that our six-week camping trip through the Soviet Union qualifies. It was fun, even exciting. It was also tough, maddening, and occasionally frightening. The USSR was the highlight of a longer, six-month journey that set us on a course of travel and living abroad that was far beyond our middle-class up-bringing and expectations.

Ours was a trip that few Americans, if any, took or were interested in taking. And that's too bad. Because if travel is broadening, travel that takes you into the heart of enemy territory is mind-bending.

Between the time I was born and the time I set foot in kindergarten, the atom bomb changed the world. I and my peers, and all those who came after us, would grow up knowing the threat of instant annihilation. I was not yet five when Winston

Churchill gave his famous speech at Westminster College in Fulton, Missouri: "From Stettin in the Baltic to Trieste in the Adriatic, an iron curtain has descended across the Continent." And so the stage was set.

The Russians—or more correctly the Soviets—were the tyrants behind that curtain. They stole into our dreams and charged our young lives with fear. America and the west were, of course, the good guys, the heroes struggling to contain evil while protecting the pure in heart.

Happily, as an adult in the early 70s I was no longer susceptible to bad dreams and propaganda—theirs or ours. But Russia had fascinated me for years; I wanted see the vast landscapes, admire the onion-domed churches, walk the cities of Tolstoy and Dostoevsky. Our visit let me do that. My husband, Ray, wanted adventure, and he got that. More importantly, we wanted to experience—as much as was possible for three naive Americans in six short weeks—how people in the Soviet Union, "our enemies," lived. And we wanted to share that knowledge with our eleven-year-old daughter, Jennifer. We wanted her to know that our enemies are just like us.

Our weeks in the Union of Soviet Socialist Republics (USSR) offered a stark comparison between life in a totalitarian state and life in a free state. But the fear and laughter we shared with our Soviet acquaintances afforded no such comparison—it was equally real and equally heartfelt. What counted was what we shared as human beings: the desire to live, love, work, perhaps to raise a family, without overbearing worry or threat of war. We just went about fulfilling those desires in different ways. Governments, economic systems, and religions all contributed to our differences, just as today they feed fear of the Other. A fear that tyrants and terrorists will always effectively cultivate.

When the Berlin Wall came down and the Soviet Union collapsed in 1989 we all cheered, still unbelieving while we watched it happen. And bit by bit the memories of that long-ago trip began to take on new meaning. Freed, perhaps, from the weight of history, they felt lighter and more valuable as they shifted and sorted themselves into anecdotes and ideas.

My memories were considerably aided by the several hundred photographs and many audio tapes made while traveling. Sadly, Ray's personal journal went missing in our last move, but I had mine and Jennifer's to draw on, and Ray's living memory.

My several hundred books on Russia and the Soviet Union were gone too, subject to too many moves. I kept a few favorites, and in some cases I was able to find new copies or new books; all was not lost. I have depended heavily on Hedrick Smith's 1976 book, *The Russians,* for its detailed and well-documented look at many aspects of Soviet life. Rereading it brought back so many memories. Vladimir Bukovsky's book, *To Build a Castle,* stood in for all the dissident literature I had lost over time, but I can't think of another that would serve as well. And Andrei Amalrik's *Will the Soviet Union Survive Until 1984?* reminded me of all the fear, late-night arguments, and hopes associated with that idea.

I want to thank Dr. Emil Draitser, the editor of *Forbidden Laughter (Soviet Underground Jokes)* for giving permission to quote his book extensively. Political humor was a critical but dangerous release valve for the Soviets, and jokes passed secretly, from friend to trustworthy friend. These jokes were smuggled by Draitser out of Russia in the early

70s. They add a dimension of cultural understanding I would be hard pressed to otherwise provide.

This book would not have been written without the encouragement and help of many. I wish to thank members of my writing group for their ongoing and cheerful support: Jan Hay, Anne Magnus, Sue Stafford, and Beverly Tobias. Thanks to Joanne McLennan, Meg Mitchell, Annette Mørk, and Nadine Fiedler who read and commented on the manuscript. Nadine also edited, for which I am especially grateful. It is a better book because of them all. Joanne McLennan drew the wonderful map of our trip and has my heartfelt appreciation for her effort and talent. And finally, big thank yous to my daughter, Jennifer, who read, commented, and contributed her own memories; and to my husband, Ray, without whose unending support (and cooking) this would never have been written.

No book is without its failures and flaws, and this one is no exception. I have tried to be accurate in all things, but memory—even when backed by journals, tapes, and photos—is ephemeral. The views and ideas expressed here, as well as the errors, are strictly my own.

CAMPING WITH THE COMMUNISTS

Question to Radio Armenia: "What is the definition of the Supreme Soviet of the USSR?"

Answer: "The Supreme Soviet is a collective organ of Soviet authority, consisting of two types of people: those who are absolutely incapable of anything, and those who are capable of absolutely everything." [1]

★ ★ ★ ★ ★

BEGINNINGS

THE MOSCOW AIR is smoggy, humid, and hot, but it doesn't matter; we have much to discuss and the park is quiet. There are few people about and no one follows us. Here, our Russian hosts assure us, we can speak freely. They take comfort in this because they have many questions.

It is August, 1977, and five of us stroll along the park's graveled path, the crunch of pebbles providing a baseline for our conversation. The questions spill out—what do we do at home? How do we live and what is America really like? What is President Carter thinking, with his neutron bomb? How do I come to speak Russian? Where else will our journey take us? And how did we come to be here, in the USSR, traveling on our own?

It is Ilya who asks that question. A fit-looking man in his fifties, he is a translator for a popular Soviet magazine, *Literaturnaya Gazeta,* and much of our conversation earlier today was about English idioms and the problems of translation.

The "how?" question makes us smile because it is one we've heard throughout our long journey. How did we—a half-time secretary, a railroad clerk, and our eleven-year-old daughter—manage a six-month trip through Europe and the Soviet Union? Of course, we must be rich! Or perhaps we are academics on sabbatical? Or maybe we secretly work for the CIA? We have heard all those assumptions. But Ilya didn't assume, he just asked. "How?"

"Oh, well," I say, laughing. "It was just an idea that grew. We planned and saved—and here we are!"

"Ah," says Ilya, and after a pause, "You know, we too can have thousands of ideas, but they all die within us."

The Soviet Union was a locked society in 1977 and Ilya wasn't the only person we met who felt trapped and hopeless. Indeed, they were trapped. The totalitarian regime, led then by Leonid Breshnev, was corrupt, mismanaged, criminal, and cruel, but it was successful in at least two things: propaganda and the destruction of optimism. Even we, who carried permission to leave the Soviet Union in our pockets, found the country oppressive, and occasionally frightening. The stifling air in Moscow that day was the physical embodiment of the emotionally gray and omnipresent constraint that weighed on us, week after week.

Nevertheless, we continued to celebrate the idea that had taken us to Moscow and beyond. Ideas, we had learned, deserve our attention, and good ideas—the ones that inspire us—require care and food and water to see them through the seedling stage and into the garden. How do we encourage those ideas or prevent them, as Ilya said, from dying within us? And just how did we come to be traveling through the USSR in a Volkswagen camper-van in 1977?

As I write this, scientists at Yale, Stanford, and elsewhere are studying intentional thought. They are telling us that our bodies respond to how we think, and that visualization and intention can influence future actions. I'm aware that athletes use visualization to improve their techniques, and that sadness and anxiety can impair our immune system. Our thoughts, we are learning, have power.

None of this was known to me in the early 1970s when I found myself on hands and knees scrubbing our kitchen floor. We were living in Eugene, Oregon then, still new to the state after a move from California's Bay Area. We loved Oregon and Eugene, and we had settled in quickly. So I was not unhappy that day, but I was disenchanted with the life I saw stretching before me. The feminist revolution was gaining ground, and like other women of my generation I was encouraged by news of growing opportunities, but felt restrained by my 1950s conditioning. It was confusing. I loved my husband and small daughter and had no interest in pursuing a life without them. But still, was this all there was?

It came to me then, sitting back on my heels and admiring my work, that Life—it was capitalized in my thoughts—was not going to hand me roses or wealth or adventure. Life was not a generous uncle. If I wanted Life to be exciting I was going to have to make it so myself.

This idea now seems embarrassingly mundane, but I was young and it hit me hard. I thought—well, I'm not sure what I thought. I only knew that I'd had an epiphany—and that something, somehow, was going to change.

Over the next few months I found myself observing my life, looking for cracks in its generally smooth surface, an opening to push through some chance for change—an idea, a place, a serendipitous moment. My one year in college had left me unprepared for a career, so I would have to look elsewhere for whatever it was I wanted.

An avid reader, I had been captivated by Russia since reading an abridged version of War and Peace in high school. The landscape, the culture: it was familiar yet strange and exotic. I felt I had been there, that I knew Sonia and the samovars and the sleds and the snow. Later I read other Russian novels, seeking them out under the dome of my hometown's old Carnegie library. As an adult I remained fascinated, and as my library of books about Russia and the Soviet Union grew, I found myself wanting more.

That yearning led me to the Russian language itself and the finer points I suspected I was missing in translations. Wouldn't it be wonderful, I thought, to read Tolstoy and Dostoevsky in the original? What I might do with that skill, besides entertain myself, remained a mystery, but with my new-found belief that only I could create my life, the idea of studying Russian became more and more intriguing. We lived in Eugene, home of the University of Oregon. The U of O had a Russian and East European Studies program. I wouldn't even have to commute.

Ideas, as we shall see, are funny things. They make perfect sense to one person and sound alarming or unrealistic to another. That was what I found when I broached Ray on the subject of returning to school. Like me he was a college dropout, but he was solidly employed and had no interest in returning to school. My sudden ambition worried him. What if I found a world that excluded him? Couples grow together or they grow apart. It was not an unreasonable fear.

Seeing his concern I temporarily put the idea aside, but gently brought it out for airing whenever the time seemed right. And when I did start classes two years later Ray was incredibly supportive. My employer had agreed to let me work half days, so I spent mornings in the office as a secretary, and afternoons on campus. Returning to school as an older student (I was 33) was uncommon in 1974, and my classmates, with one exception, were much younger than I—a situation I found slightly intimidating. My Russian teacher, a brilliant but eccentric man, read 17 or 20 languages (he could never remember for sure) and could speak half that number. Our Russian language classes were two hours a day, four days a week.

It was soon clear that I was no natural at languages. Dr. B had the nasty habit of returning our daily quizzes to us in "best first" order, and it was quickly obvious who the star pupils were—not me. I spent hours every night on my Russian homework, memorizing verbs, writing exercises. Why was it so difficult? Dr. B was sympathetic. He kept telling me one day it would "click" and become obvious and easy. It never did.

Many of my other courses focused on contemporary life in the Soviet Union, and soon I was immersed in the dissident movement and press. This was the era of Sakharov and Solzhenitzyn; of Sinyavsky and *samizdat*.[2] Andrew Amalrik's thought-provoking book, *Will the Soviet Union Survive Until 1984?* seemed like science fiction. I read everything I could and my interest in the country continued to grow. It was an exciting time to be studying Russian.

During my first year back at school we watched as several close friends made major changes in their lives. One, a political science professor, moved with his wife and three young children to New Zealand for a sabbatical year. Another couple, having both earned their Ph.Ds, gave up on Oregon's rain and moved to San Diego. We envied their exciting changes and wished we had similar plans. After all, I was now 34 and Ray was 37 and oh my God, life was passing us by!

Not for long, though. One idea, one opening door, inevitably leads to another, and one day, browsing in a local bookshop, I spotted a paperback with an intriguing title: *Europe With Two Kids and a Van*. The book described a lengthy camping trip through several European countries. Wow, I thought, what a great idea.

"Look!" I said excitedly to Ray, waving the book at him. "Let's do this!"

He looked at it skeptically. "You're crazy," he said. "We can't do that. Where would we get the money? It's impossible."

I bought the book anyway.

He was right, of course. We had jobs, but almost nothing in savings. We had a ten-year-old daughter in school. We had house payments and car payments and other bills. We had a dog and two cats. We had responsibilities. We were stuck.

No, we weren't.

You always have a choice, I said. Achieving a goal is just a matter of priorities, I insisted. We just need to reset ours, I declared. Life, I protested, was not meant to consist of working and buying. I do not want, I added, to reach my deathbed only to say, "how boring."

I was annoyingly preachy and overly confident. I'm surprised I wasn't also divorced.

I insisted Ray read the book—nagged really—and when he put it off I read parts of it aloud to him. In the meantime I found a second book: I left *European Camping and Cara-vanning* lying around in obvious places. I talked up the idea to our daughter, who was reluctant to leave her friends for more than a day. And "just for fun" I started ordering travel brochures from European tourist offices (this was, of course, long before the Internet). I was convinced that somehow every obstacle could be overcome if we all wanted this badly enough.

If Ray thought he was being manipulated he didn't complain, and though he often told me I was nuts he agreed to at least talk about a trip to Europe. We knew that under his union rules he was eligible for up to a year's leave of absence. I was prepared to quit my job if I had to; the pay was higher than average but I had no emotional investment in it. The hard part, discussed endlessly, was how to pay for the kind of trip we wanted. Then, a few months into our discussions I added a new twist—my Russian studies should be put to use—we could visit the Soviet Union! It was the pure adventure of this idea that finally excited Ray.

*During one of his speeches Stalin remarked: "I am
prepared to give my blood for the cause of the working class—
drop by drop!"*

*A note was then passed up to the podium which read: "Dear
Comrade Stalin, why drag things out? Give it all at once!"*

HOW WE DID IT

IN AUGUST 1976 the three of us sat down and agreed on a departure date the following June. Committing ourselves to a six-month trip through Europe was exciting but scary. It meant drastic changes to our lifestyle and required commitment from all three of us. To help accomplish our goal we agreed on one rule: we would never use the phrase, "*if* we go to Europe." Only *when* was allowed. And we would immediately tell our friends, work colleagues, and relatives about our plans, publicly committing ourselves to the challenge. Although we didn't know it at the time, we were doing what sages and seers had been saying for centuries: declare your intentions plainly and believe your goals will be met.

We had ten months to save and plan, but three immediate decisions were critical to our success. First, to cover our mortgage we agreed to rent our house, unfurnished. Our wonderful neighbors volunteered their unused two-car garage for storage—a fine synchronicity. We contacted a rental agent and began to make those arrangements.

Second, we decided to purchase a new (1977) VW Westfalia camper van, ordering it from a local dealer for European delivery. We briefly considered buying a used van in Europe, but after learning that if we broke down in the Soviet Union we would be towed to the nearest border due to lack of parts or repair knowledge, we opted for the new and, we hoped, reliable car. To save money we ordered the basic model, without a pop-top, stove, or radio. Jennifer, still small and light, would sleep in a canvas hammock stretched across the two front seats. The van had an "ice box" that we could use for storing food, and we would purchase a small camp stove in Europe.

At that time the dollar was strong and European cars were less expensive when purchased abroad, so we planned to ship the van home and sell it after the trip, recouping, we hoped, most of our travel expenses. The van became key to our plans. It offered flexible transportation, cheap shelter, and minimal cooking facilities. And camping would be far less expensive, and far more of an adventure, than staying in hotels.

We would sell our current car—a two-year-old Volvo station wagon—and use our bikes and local bus service until departure, banking the monthly car payments, insurance, and gas costs. This was an easy decision for Ray, who was already a confirmed bicycle commuter. Jennifer walked to school. It was up to me, the driver, to adapt.

Because we would be taking our daughter out of school for the fall term, we had several meetings with her teachers and principal. She was a good student, and all agreed that the trip itself offered an unmatched learning experience. The school's only requirement was that we provide arithmetic lessons so she wouldn't fall behind in that important subject. Ray, always good with numbers, promised to take on that task.

Each of these decisions required hours of research and discussion that often left us confused and exhausted, wondering if our choices were right. We cheered when the approval came for Ray's leave of absence. I cried when we handed over the keys to the Volvo—a car I had waited long for and loved—convinced that we could never again afford a new car.

Fortunately, the Oregon winter turned out to be unusually dry, though cold and foggy. We carried groceries the four uphill blocks to home, biked to work and campus daily—which soon became an effortless habit—and walked to a nearby pizza place when we needed a break from our money-saving regime. Jennifer, enthusiastic at last, counted up the days and posted a chart on the refrigerator; together we made a daily ceremony of blacking in each square. Two weeks before Christmas we pushed a wheelbarrow down the hill to the nearest tree lot a mile away, picked out a six-foot fir and pushed it home. Challenges were frequent, and most of them were fun.

Our friends became our biggest supporters. Many of them were also neighbors, so we didn't have far to go to let off steam or share the latest update. It helped immeasurably to have supportive friends nearby, because the drudgery of scrimping and the inevitable setbacks meant we had bad days as well as good. Luckily, we three seemed to rotate through despair, so while one might moan, the other two managed to hold tight to our intention.

For those ten months, saving money was our first priority, and though we were often tempted by the plethora of things and events around us, we soon learned to prioritize.

The phrase, "Would you rather (eat out, see a movie, go to the beach, fill in the blank) or go to Europe?" quickly became a household joke, but Europe almost always won. Ten months, after all, was a finite length of time, and missing a blockbuster movie or a good restaurant meal was a minor blip in the larger scheme. As the days slipped away and our goal drew nearer, our plans—and the hope that we would actually succeed—began to congeal into reality. In January we visited a travel agent and began the wearying exercise of obtaining Soviet Union visas.

Few of us plan trips these days without resorting to the Internet for reviews, advice, photos, and reservations. Home computers were still rare in 1977, and there was no Internet, nor smart phones, digital cameras, video games, Kindles, or iPads. Telephones were tied to the wall, and television—with its three networks and limited cable—was the epitome of home entertainment. Information about destinations had to be sought in books and libraries, from individual tourist offices, from travel agents, and from friends who had gone before. Knowledge about the very closed Soviet Union was limited to scholarly books and articles, political analyses, broadcast news, and a few popular books, like *The Russians,* by Hedrick Smith. The iron curtain was firmly in place.

Planning for the Soviet Union

Although the complete trip would take us in a circle through 17 countries, it was planning for the Soviet Union that took most of our time and attention. It took six months and eight kinds of documents to enter the Soviet Union and travel independently—that is, without a group or an accompanying Intourist[3] guide. Visa requirements were tedious and exacting, and all expenses had to be paid in advance. The most difficult task was producing the stipulated day-by-day itinerary of our proposed trip, based on a map provided by Intourist. This was not a true road map but a graphic depiction showing only the few roads we were authorized to drive on, the cities we could visit, and the location of gas stations (very few).

The permitted roads were all in the far western part of the country and included a single north-south route stretching from the Finnish border through Leningrad to Moscow, and south to Yerevan, Armenia. Extensions from this highway went west to Estonia, Poland, and Romania, with side trips to Yalta and Odessa. From Tbilisi, Georgia, one could travel west to the Black Sea and up the coast, rejoining the main north-south highway. The map also showed roads east out of Moscow, to Yaroslav and Suzdal, but it turned out we were not allowed to take them.

To reach a decision about our route we talked to everyone we could think of who had traveled to the Soviet Union, including most of my professors. No one, it appeared, had driven and camped the way we wanted to, but we did find one person, a friend of a friend in Chicago, who had camped for two nights near Leningrad. We picked up the phone and called her, but her experience was limited and not much help. Only her final words left an impression: "The toilets are terrible!"

So, guessing about road conditions and trusting in a limited way the brochures provided by Intourist, we planned a trip that would take us from the Finnish border to Leningrad (St. Petersburg), west to Tallinn, Estonia, and back to Leningrad, then south through Novgorod, Moscow, Kursk, and Kharkov to Georgia and the Black Sea coast. From there we had to retrace our route north to Kharkov before heading west to Kiev, and into Romania. We asked to camp through the entire trip but Intourist arbitrarily put us in motels and other accommodations eleven nights. No reason was given; we suspected they just wanted more money, but in the end we were grateful for the change of pace the hotel and other stops afforded us.

Our trip through the Soviet Union would cover 3,812 miles (6,135 kilometers) in 39 days, an average of 193 miles per day. By the time we knew we had been far too optimistic about Soviet roads and travel, we were dodging potholes and following slow trucks, and it was much too late to turn back.

Looking back I have to laugh at our optimism. Even Russians we met along the way shook their heads and said worryingly, "Oh, that's too long," when we told them we would stay six weeks. When asked why, they would change the subject.

Our Soviet visas arrived just three weeks before our scheduled departure date. In a last minute hitch our charter flight was cancelled, so we booked a Pan Am flight out of Seattle that set us down in London. From there a short flight took us to Brussels and our waiting VW camper. We were actually on our way.

From Belgium we toured Germany, England, Wales, and Scotland; then it was back to England where we ferried to Holland. From there we drove north to Scandinavia.

We awoke the morning of July, 25, 1977, in a campground in Finland, near the sea. We had spent several days there, gathering the additional food and other supplies we'd need for our journey through the Soviet Union. Finland was far and away the most expensive country we'd visited. Our $25-a-day-budget—tight in the best of circumstances— didn't go far here. We'd laughed at ourselves a night or two before, when the scent of sausages roasting over a neighboring camper's fire had us all salivating. Finnish sausages were not in our budget.

Our visas stated that we had to appear at the Soviet border on this day and no other. If we couldn't make it, too bad. Our USSR entry and exit were the only firm dates in our six-month journey; all our planning had circled around this day.

"Comrade Rabinowitz, why weren't you present at the last meeting of the Communist Party?"

"No one told me that it would be the last one. If I had known that, I would have come with my whole family . . ."

THE BORDER

IT'S RAINING HARD when we leave our campground and drive to the Finnish-Soviet border. First stop, a guard house with two Finnish guards, who examine and stamp our passports without comment and open the gate for us. Then a second gate, with two more guards. Then a drive across a plowed and empty stretch of land, and in the distance tall wire fences and wooden towers guarding the Soviet border. Then two Soviet soldiers in heavy coats, who examine our passports and wave us on. Soon we're in a line of three cars. The wait begins.

Crossing borders can be a tedious and somewhat nerve-wracking experience. Innocent you may be, but the presence of sullen guards waving machine guns can leave you shaking in your shoes. In this case we were entering a country that had imbued our childhood with anxiousness. This was the enemy from whom we hid under school desks during drills; who threatened to bury us; who had me believing—riding a

San Francisco city bus in October, 1962—that my life might end before I reached home. The Soviet Union was the evil enigma whose existence had dominated U.S. foreign policy through eight presidencies.

Yet here we were with our eleven-year-old daughter, waiting in line at a border crossing, trying to be patient, wondering what to expect, but confident we would get through it. We watch as the cars ahead of us are searched, as the driver and passengers get out, enter and leave the building, pace, wait.

Directly ahead of us is a single woman in a car with French plates. We watch as the guards examine the car, poking long metal rods into every crevice and hole they can find. Suddenly the woman starts yelling. *Non! Non!* The guards insist, *Da! Da!* There is much hubbub, other guards come out of the building, mill around, discuss. The woman lets go a torrent of angry French. The Soviets, it appears, are preparing to slit her car seats with a knife. She threatens to turn around and go back to Finland. This bothers them not at all, but her defiance and firmness does defeat them (a powerful lesson for us) and she climbs into the car, seats intact, and drives off. We're next.

We quickly realize that having our daughter with us will be an advantage. Families, it appears, are less threatening to the state than individuals, and children are highly regarded. Her presence doesn't halt the ridiculous search that takes place, but it does make the guards a little more friendly. They actually permit her to wander around the guard post while our car is searched.

"What is this?" says a young soldier, holding a slim blue paperback with a Russian title. He has been examining all our books.

"It's a textbook," I say. "I'm a student of Russian language and I'm reading it, but it's difficult." We had decided it would be best if officials didn't know I spoke some Russian, but in this case I'm found out.

"It's about Russia?" he asks, flipping through the pages.

"Yes, it's a history."

He leans against the bus and begins to read. During most of our time at the border crossing he stands and reads his own country's history and I know that it differs dramatically from what he was taught. I long to ask what he thinks but am reluctant to bring his attention back to us, so I leave him alone.

Other guards search the bus with their long wires, probing any hole the frame offers while ignoring our baggage, camera bags, even the cupboards of the bus, though they open the doors and briefly peer in. They are looking for black market rubles, Bibles, or other "illegal" literature; drugs maybe. One carefully examines our fruit and takes away a small houseplant I'd been babying. We are there about two hours and though it is stressful and tiresome, all goes smoothly. Finally, we are told to move on, but our passports haven't been returned. I ask one of the female guards about it and she shrugs, looking at me with what I can only describe as hatred, which shakes me deeply. Is this what it's going to be like? I wonder.

At last, our belongings are re-stowed, our passports are returned, and we're on the road.

"Look, Jennifer," says Ray, "there's a Russian cow! And a Russian dog!" "And a Russian house," I chime in. Thus do we convince ourselves that we've actually done this, that we're driving east along a bumpy two-lane road into the

Union of Soviet Socialist Republics—on our own without a tour or even a guide, toward an adventure few Americans have experienced. I marvel at our accomplishment, knowing that only determination and the power of an idea has brought us here.

Before long we're stopped by a group of young boys who dash out of the shrubbery and hold hands across the road. They want chewing gum. We dig into our supply and hand it out. This happens again, and then again. Between chewing-gum stops we are twice passed by cars honking their horns while a grinning and slightly menacing passenger leans out the window and waves ruble bills at us. Who would dare buy black-market rubles this close to the border? I wonder, as we wave them off. Later a taxi stops us and again the driver wants to sell rubles.[4] When we say no, he asks if we have anything to sell. No again. So he wishes us a safe journey, gets back in his taxi and drives off. All this is fun and fascinating; it's exciting to be heading into this hidden world so unlike our own.

We are well prepared too. In addition to our passports, visas, and international driver's licenses, we carry a camping card, an auto insurance card, a signed customs declaration (which states that we have no guns, Bibles, anti-Soviet tapes, films, or publications; no drugs, diamonds, lottery tickets, pornography, or live pigeons—who knew?); two signed currency certificates, a form pledging that we will not leave or sell our car, an official hand-written itinerary, four tourist cards—one for each type of overnight stay (camping, hotel, cabin, motel); 117 prepaid housing coupons, one for each overnight times three; and about 145 prepaid five-liter gasoline coupons.

We are told to keep strict records of any currency exchanges and to plan on showing receipts for all purchases when leaving the country.[5] As we roll away from the Intourist office in Vyborg, near the Finnish border, we have about 275 pieces of paper to keep track of. We've only driven a few miles and already we are tightly enmeshed in the incomprehensible Soviet bureaucracy.

Northern Russia is flat and green, part of a wide plain marked by lakes and forests known as the taiga. Lake Ladoga, the largest in Europe at 107,000 square miles, lies just 60 miles east of Vyborg. If we were in any other country at least one of us would say, "Lets go see that big lake," but since there is no approved route to Lake Ladoga our only option is to keep going. There are no mountains here, only a water-rich, wooded plain that rolls for miles toward the Ural mountains, the geographic boundary dividing east from west. From the Finnish border to Moscow we will see a rise of only 400 feet.

But despite the sameness of the northern scenery, boredom is never a threat. The panorama that rolls past our windows is filled with people, and it is there we find the variety, texture, and character missing in the landscape.

Our immediate impression is of shabbiness and hardship, a view that gains validity with each day of travel. The powerful country that has kept us cowering turns out to be a kind of Potemkin's village[6]—a grandiose false front hiding a peasant's reality.

Before long we pass a wooden tower beside the road. I look back and see an officer leaning out the tower window, a phone to his ear as he follows our car with his eyes. So now we know they are keeping track of us.

It takes only a few hours of driving to realize our van is a major source of curiosity, and we try to accustom ourselves to being on the receiving end of constant, overt stares. People stop work to turn to watch us go past. Sometimes they run across fields to get a better view, so apparently strange is our vehicle. Passengers in passing cars turn and stare while we in turn examine the few Russian cars we see: mostly Zhigulis—Russian Fiats—and the slightly sleeker, slightly larger Volgas. Most look well used.

We make good time until we near Leningrad, where we confront what will become the greatest traffic impediment throughout our long trip: slow trucks. They resemble WWII army trucks or dump trucks; almost all have a single open bed. In my memory they are brown, but our photos show the cabs as pale blue; it is the rear of the truck that is brown. Our days will be spent following these underpowered trucks, sometimes dodging what drops off them, seeking to pass and finally passing, only to come up behind another slow truck.

Our first overnight stay is at a campground in Repino, 27 miles (44km) north of Leningrad. Our *American's Tourist Manual for the USSR* [7] (which makes everything sound much better than it is) tells us that Repino is known for its seaside resorts, which we never see, that 8,000 people live here, and that it was once a Finnish city, Kuokkala. The nearer we come to Repino the more nervous I am. The roads are not marked well; what if we can't find the campground? What if we can't work through the anticipated red tape? Will my two years of Russian be sufficient to the task?

My worry, of course, is wasted. We easily find the campground, drive past the two old men in street clothes guarding the gate, check in with the administration office, show our camping cards, hand over our passports, and are directed to a site.

The Repino campground was a good place to begin, for it was one of the worst we saw. The field was weedy and bumpy—we had a hard time finding a level parking spot. Overhead lights would shine all night and two uniformed policemen patrolled. And, according to other campers, four or five plainclothes policemen were also on site.

When we climbed out of the van to explore we found a *bufe* (buffet) that would be replicated in nearly every campground. It might stand alone or be connected to a larger cafe, but inevitably its contents were never-changing: a table or two surrounded by ubiquitous white plastic chairs, and a refrigerated cabinet holding cheese on bread, fatty sausage on bread, caviar (but rarely), *kefir*, champagne, wine, beer. Sometimes there would be vodka, sometimes Pepsi Cola—the only U.S. import we found. Sometimes there were two varieties of cheese or sausage, and sometimes eggs. But mostly it was a depressing and limited collection of tired cheese and greasy sausage.

We bought a couple of beers for later and headed to the restrooms to check the facilities. Alas, they also were tired and depressing and unclean, with "squat" toilets and dirty floors. Anyone wearing long pants had to roll them up before entering, and then perform a jiggling little dance to keep the flies away. This was our first experience with squat toilets, a good indication of how naive we still were.

My first question on arrival at any campground was always "Are there hot showers?" and in this case there were. But when Jennifer and I peered in we decided we'd pass. Ray bravely walked down during the posted evening hours and showered, while an old, toothless man shoveled coal into a boiler.

"The water," Ray said, "barely dribbled out." The next day, as Jennifer and I were heading to the toilets, we passed a Polish man exiting who muttered, "Primitive. Very primitive!"

Our fellow campers were a wonderful source of information, always ready to share experiences and recommend or steer us away from restaurants or places to see. And since routes and campgrounds were limited—especially for westerners—we often crossed paths. We soon came to rely on a network of camper gossip for news about experiences other campers were having (run-ins with the police, for example), and how good or bad the next campground on our itinerary might be. In Repino we were quickly warned off the water, which was "Very bad, it will make you sick." Fortunately, we had filled the van's water tank in Finland. We also had water purification tablets that we used throughout our Soviet journey.

The Repino campground housed visitors from Poland, Czechoslovakia, East Germany, West Germany, Sweden, Norway, Holland, Italy, Australia, New Zealand, Egypt, and America. We were happy to meet other Americans, but disappointed to learn they were there only to see the Hermitage Museum, and would return to Finland in two days.

Soviet citizens were also camping in Repino, but they were separated from the foreigners. This wasn't always the case, but it happened frequently. Even when it was the rule, the Russians and other Soviets managed to find their way into "foreigner" territory to talk and ask questions. And we were just as eager to meet and talk with them.

After we settled in Ray insisted we walk into town, though I would have been happy to stay safely in the campground. Repino wasn't a pretty place, but we found everything worth seeing. We stumbled onto a wooden shelter that turned out to be a beer stand, and the bartender immediately asked Ray, who was wearing jeans, to exchange pants with him. His pleas continued throughout our hour-long stay but there was nothing we could do. We had been warned again and again not to sell things or deal in black market rubles, and at this point we were determined not to do so.

There were three or four other customers, all men, and we were soon engaged in conversation, with me working to translate, answering their questions and asking our own, and laughing at joint misunderstandings. Every traveler has had many such conversations; they could almost be scripted: where do you live, what is your job, how much money do you make, how much did your car (or house) cost, what is it like in America? And, of course, our fellow beer drinkers wondered why we were visiting and how long we would stay. Our questions, in turn, were similar. Generally, such conversations, if they go on long enough, veer into other areas of life, often politics, but in the Soviet Union people did not openly speak about their ideas or beliefs. Fear or habit kept them silent.

At some point the bartender gave me a tomato, a customer bought Jennifer ice cream, and a wizened little man, whom I liked greatly, pulled a small dried fish out of his pocket and gave it to me. I wasn't much of a fish eater then and I stood there looking and feeling dumb, with no idea what to do. I also wondered how long it had been in his pocket. Another man laughed, took it from me, broke off the head and tail, peeled off the skin, and gave it back. I ate it and it was good.

This generosity was typical of Russians, and we would find it everywhere. We surely appeared wealthy to them, and to us they looked poor. But no matter what we did or said, gifts were thrust upon us throughout the trip, from precious black pepper wadded in newsprint to an electric samovar from someone's sideboard. We had brought small gifts to give away: gum, pens, cigarettes, small notebooks, postcards, etc., but they were soon gone and we had little to give in return. We were frequently embarrassed because no matter how often we said "No, thank you," our pleas went unheard.

Mao Tse-Tung sent the following telegram to Nikita Khruschchev: "HUNGER IN CHINA STOP PLEASE SEND FOODSTUFFS STOP."

Khrushchev responded to this with: "TIGHTEN BELTS STOP."

The following day Mao Tse-Tung sent the following telegram to Khrushchev: "PLEASE SEND BELTS STOP."

LENINGRAD

THE NEXT DAY we got up early and drove into Leningrad for our three-hour tour of the city. This was to be typical, for included in our camping fees was a city tour, either by bus when available, or in our own car with an Intourist guide. At first we welcomed the tours and enjoyed the sights, but as the trip wore on we began to ask guides to take us to markets where we could buy fruit and vegetables, instead of showing us the local war memorial or another statue of Lenin or Pushkin.

Leningrad (formerly and now St. Petersburg) was high on my list of places to see. We would spend five nights here—two in the Repino campground and three in the Leningrad hotel, with a side trip to Estonia sandwiched between. I couldn't believe I was in Tolstoy's St. Petersburg, and we eagerly joined the American couple and our new Dutch friends on the bus. But the Leningrad we saw from its windows was no longer Tolstoy's city. I wasn't disappointed, change was expected, but it made me sad that such a beautiful city could be brought so low. The grand buildings, the monuments, all stood in their places, but their façades were faded and shabby, their glory diminished.

There were many structures, of course, that were historically important and worthy of upkeep (they drew international tourists with hard currency). These were well kept, shiny with gold trim and new paint, and serene in their magnificent settings. The Smolny Institute was one of these. Once a school for "Noble Maidens," built in 1806–08, it was the first of several educational establishments for women. Suzanne Massey writes in *Land of the Firebird* that the girls were taught "modern languages (French, English and German) followed by geography, religion, ancient and modern history." And she adds, "Most startling for foreigners, including John Quincy Adams, then the American Ambassador, their program also included physics and mathematics." [8]

The Institute traditionally operated under the patronage of the Russian Empress so it is, perhaps, a bit ironic that Vladimir Lenin placed the Bolshevik headquarters here during the October Revolution of 1917.

The gigantic Winter Palace, official residence of the Russian Tsars from 1732 to 1917, still extended its grand, green-and-white baroque façade along the Neva River, an inescapable monument to wealth and power, but also to architecture and art. It contains a portion of the famous Hermitage Museum (my Soviet tourist manual reports it has over 322 exhibition halls with more than two million exhibits) and like the Smolny it was freshly painted and well cared for.

In the 19th century St. Petersburg was a glamorous and sophisticated city, home to writers such as Pushkin,

Dostoevsky, and Gogol; musicians like Mussorgsky, Glinka, and Rimsky-Korsakov; artists such as Diaghilev and his amazing creation, the Ballets Russes, and of course the House of Fabergé. Peter Carl Fabergé oversaw seven hundred craftsmen and created extraordinary "objects of fantasy," including the famous Imperial Easter eggs.

The city itself was the creation of Peter the Great (1672–1725), carved out of swamp and islands at the mouth of the Neva. It is relatively new for a city; the first digging was done May 16, 1703, beginning a monumental effort that brought misery and death to many of the hundreds of thousands who labored on its construction. And since few people chose to live there, Peter used force, bringing first his relatives and then other wealthy citizens from Moscow. Most hated it. But to Peter, a man in love with the sea, it was perfection. "I cannot help writing you from this paradise," he wrote to a friend; "truly we live here in heaven." [9]

Peter desperately wanted Russia to reflect the sophistication and modernism he had seen during his "incognito" tour of Europe, and to that end he forced dramatic changes on his people. He forbade the wearing of traditional caftans and forced men to shave their beards, which for many had religious significance. He introduced education reform, established hospitals and museums, created Russia's first navy, and completely revamped the army, creating a permanent officer class.

Tsar Peter's push to "Europeanize" Russia created a tension in the country that still exists, but the city he created is a worthy monument to a ruler who was intelligent, curious, active, and ruthless.

It would take others to build on Peter's work and make it the exotic, exciting place it would become. In *Peter the*

Great: His Life and World, author Robert Massie describes it thus: "With its merging of wind and water and cloud, its 150 arching bridges linking the nineteen islands, its golden spires and domes, its granite columns and marble obelisks, St. Petersburg would be called the Babylon of the Snows and the Venice of the North." [10] In the 18th and 19th centuries wealthy Europeans flocked to Russia to partake of the magic emanating from this northern city.

And in 1977 Leningrad, the grand monuments and imposing architecture still called for an affluent, cosmopolitan citizenry, as bedecked in gaudy glory as the landmark buildings themselves. But instead, the city appeared seedy and run down, and the people looked glum and discouraged.

After the bus tour we spent the afternoon wandering the famous Nevsky Prospekt and the streets that crossed it, content to look and look and look. We admired the canals, the riverfront, the baroque architecture, and the pre-revolutionary monuments—the Bronze Horseman by Falconet, and the Triumphal Arch by Rossi, to name just two. We wandered through the government-run shops (all stores in the Soviet Union were owned and operated by the government) and were increasingly surprised by the lack of goods. The clothes in the windows were beautiful, stylish, and well made, but they were not the clothes of the people we saw on the streets. These finer goods would go to those with *blat*—influence of one kind or another. *Blat* operated on all levels of Soviet society and was essential to living the good life. Members of the Politburo had a lot of *blat* and lived extremely well.

The Russians on the street wore clothes that mimicked western styles—mini skirts and bell-bottoms in 1977—but to my eyes they looked cheap and ill-fitting.

At some point we wandered into Dom Knigi (The House of Books) in the old Singer Sewing Machine building, with its high ceilings and ornate fixtures. Almost instantly I was approached by a young woman wanting to buy the denim skirt I was wearing. I said no, and seeing her disappointment felt terrible, but believed I had no other choice. She kept insisting, coaxing me with "please, please" and offering more and more money. She desperately wanted what to me was a well-worn, no frills, wrap-around denim skirt. As people turned to stare I grew embarrassed and anxious. I repeated "No, sorry" several more times, while slowly backing away. Then I turned, searched for Ray and Jennifer, and we quickly left.

Writing about this incident in my journal I said, "I have the impression of being free and on the outside, while they're inside looking out." It wasn't a feeling I liked, but I would come to know it well.

The Dom Knigi scene would repeat itself hundreds of times. The Soviets were desperate for anything Western and we could have sold everything in the bus and all the clothes off our backs many times over. Of course they wanted our audio cassettes and tape recorder, but also our shoes, handbags, soap, perfume, kitchen pans, even Ray's eyeglasses. Requests to change money, highly illegal, were also a daily refrain. In the beginning this was fun and a good excuse to speak, even briefly, with Russians, but as the days passed it began to wear on all of us, inevitably becoming a frustrating and irritating pattern. We tried hard to avoid losing our patience and sense of humor.

But now, on this day, we are still excited and curious and enjoying all we see, and here is a bread shop offering good-looking rolls and heavy loaves of bread. Like most of the shops along this thoroughfare the government bread shop is anachronistically housed in a building that to my untrained eye shares the style of the city's grander edifices, an 18th and 19th century baroque montage. The wooden floors lost their luster long ago, but the high ceilings, decorative trim, and surprisingly-out-of-place crystal chandelier all remain as telling reminders of other times.

We buy a loaf of bread. This is our first lesson in Russian shopping, distinctly different from shopping at home. It works like this: First you stand in a line—this one had eight to ten people—to choose your product, which for us usually meant pointing at it across a counter. The clerk then writes your purchase on a slip of paper which you carry to the cashier. But first you must wait in her line, equally as long. After reaching the front of the line you hand the slip of paper and your rubles to the cashier. Most often an abacus is used to calculate your purchase. Rarely, we saw a calculator used, but apparently they weren't thought reliable; the results were always checked with an abacus.

In due course the cashier hands you a receipt and you return to the end of the first line. After another long wait, you hand over your receipt and receive your purchase in return.

This awkward, multi-step process makes shopping a kind of endurance test, and since almost all goods are scarce, including groceries, it means a good deal of time is wasted just getting the daily necessities. It wasn't long before we learned to work as a team, with me standing in one line and Ray in another, passing the precious bits of paper back and forth. And we weren't the only ones.

Most Russian women, eight-five percent of whom worked, spent much of their free time shopping for necessities. It was assumed most women spent two hours daily waiting in lines.[11] Occasionally we saw lines spring from nowhere as an offering of shoes, or shoelaces, or whatever, appeared in a shop. Lines grew quickly out of curiosity and need, and purchases were often made even when need was nonexistent. Items could always be resold.

From the bread shop we returned to our van and headed back to the campground. Our minds were filled with all we had seen, and as we drove we talked, sorting through the experiences, processing what we had learned. It had been fun but tiring, and we had a long drive ahead of us the next day—222 miles (358 kilometers) to Tallinn, capital of the Estonian Republic and our first stop outside Russia itself.

We left Repino the next morning, glad to say goodbye to the uneven field and the filthy toilets. Though the Soviet government insisted we drive only on designated roads, they made it difficult to comply. Road signs were rare and in the countryside often nonexistent. This lack of signage was frustrating and it frequently angered me. (Since I was the navigator it also caused me to swear a lot: "If they're so damned anxious for us to stay on their f--king roads why don't they put up f--king signs?") We frequently got lost.

On this morning we had to get through Leningrad on the main highway and make a turn to the west. We turned onto a road that looked promising. It was at least a highway, but we still weren't sure it was the right one. Help arrived in the form of a hitchhiker, a short, gray-haired woman wearing a white lace blouse and gray skirt, who waved us down.

I rolled down my window and said, "Hello, can you please tell us if this is the road to Tallinn?" She smiled and nodded a little vaguely and I was uncertain whether she actually knew. I asked her again and got the same indeterminate answer.

"Are you going far in this direction?" she asked, pointing west. "*Da*, to *Tallinn*," I said, emphasizing the word.

She quickly rattled off a string of Russian, most of which I understood. It was clear she wanted a ride and equally clear we would give her one. I got out and opened the sliding side door for her and she climbed in. She was so short she could stand in the bus without crouching, and before she sat down she asked, "Where are you from?" When I told her we were Americans she looked slightly alarmed but she sat down anyway, on the bench seat beside Jennifer, who quickly made room by moving her books and assorted papers to the rear of the bus.

As soon as our guest was seated Ray put the bus in gear and we took off down the road, while I turned in my seat and prepared to have a conversation. I introduced each of us and asked her name. Anna. She said she was on her way to visit her daughter and grandchildren; she didn't know how far it was. I showed her the map we had purchased in Leningrad, but it meant nothing to her.[12] And before we could go further she must ask a question. "Of course," I said.

"Do Americans want war?"

"Oh, no!" I said. "No, not at all!" Then I translated for Ray and Jennifer who chimed in with their own vehement denials. Anna smiled and seemed content with this, and we went on our way.

It didn't surprise us that she asked this question—we were acutely aware of the American missiles pointed our way—but it made us sad that war might be the first thing people thought of when we met. It was understandable though, for unless she secretly listened to the forbidden and frequently blocked radio broadcasts by the BBC or Voice of America, she would receive no news other than what her government chose to tell her, and much of that was lies.

There were almost no foreign newspapers or magazines available to ordinary citizens, though some communist papers and nonpolitical books made it into the country (Dr. Spock's baby book for instance) and, with the exception of northern Estonia, there was no foreign television. The United States was the declared enemy, and mutually assured destruction (MAD) was the justification. Like other tyrants before them, the Soviet leaders knew it was easier to keep people tightly controlled when truth was hidden, fear flourished, and an enemy was at the gate.

We drove with Anna several hours and I worked to keep up a conversation, translating questions from my companions. She was a simple woman and didn't have much to tell us, nor did she ask a lot of questions. Around noon Jennifer decided she was hungry so she got out the peanut butter we'd brought from home and made sandwiches. Peanut butter was unknown in the Soviet Union, and on tasting this American staple Anna wrinkled up her nose and gave us the Russian expression for yuck, which made us all laugh. It reminded me of our reaction to that Australian delicacy, Vegemite. Soon after, we reached her destination, a small, plain wooden house beside the highway. She climbed out, a child came running, and they waved goodbye as we drove away. She no doubt had a lot to tell that evening.

President John Kennedy and Nikita Khrushchev ran a foot-race. The next day the Soviet newspapers published the following account:

"Our beloved Nikita Sergeevich Khrushchev won a very respectable second place in the race. The American president barely managed to arrive at the finish line in next-to-last position."

TALLINN, ESTONIA

TALLINN, IN THE Soviet Republic of Estonia, lies just 50 miles (81 kilometers) south of Helsinki, Finland, across the Gulf of Finland. During World War II it was occupied by the Soviets in 1939, then taken by Nazi Germany, then retaken again by the USSR in 1944. Estonia has the misfortune to straddle that invisible line that has long separated east from west, and its history is one of invasions and shifting alliances.

I still have the little tourist book we picked up in Tallinn. It was printed by Progress Publishers in Moscow and is undated. The text is in six languages, for Tallinn remained a popular tourist spot even under Soviet rule. A trip by ferry from Helsinki to Tallinn was especially popular with people who enjoyed the cheap alcohol they could buy in Estonia. But there was much to recommend the city besides alcohol.

According to the tour book, Tallinn was first marked on a map in 1154, by an Arab scientist named Mohammed Idrisi. "It was," says the text, "a city of master craftsmen and merchants . . . and attracted numerous traders, travelers and scientists." This is true, for it was an important link in the chain of cities controlled by the Hanseatic League, a confederation of merchants who cooperated in the late Middle Ages to protect their trade routes.

What isn't so true is how the book describes the current (1977) state of Estonia. After declaring that the city has "thrice reached its heyday" it describes these as the 15th century, when many of the lovely old buildings were built; the 18th century, "when Estonia acceded to Russia," and the glorious present, "as the proud capital of the Estonian Soviet Socialist Republic."

This is typical of the propaganda that filled Soviet tourist brochures, and was frequently parroted by our tour guides. We quickly tired of the "great, greater, greatest" message and soon quit listening. Most Estonians would disagree that their "heyday" moments occurred under Russian and Soviet rule, though our guide cheerfully told us the Soviets had been "invited" by the Estonians to rule their country. Despite her message we knew that a free-government-in-exile had been headquartered in Sweden since 1944, awaiting the day Estonia would be free of Soviet dominance. That happened August 20, 1999, when, after the collapse of the Soviet Union, Estonia returned to being an independent state. In 2004 it joined the European Union.

But we are not there yet. It's still 1977 and we're still bumbling along, driving our VW bus through the cobbled streets of this beautiful little city, searching for the campground we've been assigned. The buildings are of stone, ancient but beautifully cared for; the 15th century town hall is lovely. The city has a definite Germanic feel to it, with steeply peaked roofs and high, narrow steeples. There is even a castle, called Toompea, where the Estonian Council of Ministers has its offices.

The people too, look different. They appear more prosperous and happier than their Leningrad counterparts, and are better dressed. They are better informed as well, because they receive two television channels from Helsinki. There are certainly more goods in the shops. Tallinn will be the site of the 1980 Olympics sailing events, and the government is spending money repairing and repainting, and building new facilities too.

Surrounding the old city are blocky high-rise apartments, ugly in their gray stolidness. These huge apartment blocks mar the outskirts of every Soviet city. Such housing, we are told, "begins and ends in vodka," and in many instances the vodka shows in sagging balconies, uneven windows, and misaligned façades. Still, the buildings are a blessing to the thousands and thousands of people who have been sharing communal apartments for years and who now have a place of their own.

Eventually, we find the campground and settle in. We are again separated from the Soviets. But the facilities are a great improvement over Repino, and the *bufe* actually has small, individual-sized bottles of orange juice. It's the first juice we've seen since entering the USSR. We're thrilled and greedily buy all five.

There is a velodrome near the campground and Ray— an avid cyclist— immediately heads there, while I prepare to call Jan, an Estonian ship captain we had met six weeks earlier in Horsens, Denmark. I am not optimistic, though he did give us his number.

We met Jan and his first mate on a quiet, overcast Sunday in June. We were driving along the waterfront in Horsens looking for something to do.

"Oh look," I said, "there's a Russian ship. I wonder what they're doing here."

"Let's go say hello," said Ray.

"Are you kidding? We can't just drop by and say hello. They'd probably have us arrested."

"Well, I'm going to give it a try."

I have learned to be quiet when Ray is determined so I just shrugged and settled in to watch. I was sure it would lead nowhere.

Five minutes later he strolled up the pier and hollered "*dobroe ytra*" [good morning] to two men standing on the uppermost deck. "*Dobroe den*" [good day] shouted one of them. Ray followed with "We are Americans and we're on our way to visit your country!"

"Would you like to come aboard?" (This in English.)

"What?"

"Come aboard!"

By now I am out of the car too, with Jennifer on my heels. Of course we would go aboard, but for what? We were flabbergasted. Not knowing what to expect, but excited and curious, we climbed the steel gangplank and were met by a worried-looking young sailor. I told him in Russian that we'd been invited aboard.

"Wait here."

He was soon back, motioning us to follow him up three flights of metal stairs and into a room that turned out to be the captain's dining room. We were invited to sit down by a blond man wearing a casual, short-sleeved shirt. It was the ship's captain, Jan. And then came the inevitable offer of a drink. Beer? Champagne? Or perhaps a little cognac? Our protestations that it was too early in the day got us nowhere so we settled on a beer (and pineapple juice and a huge bowl of Russian chocolates for Jennifer) and we were soon asking general questions about the ship. It was 11 a.m.

Jan, like all ship captains, spoke English, and told us about his ship, which was in Horsens to buy 1,300 tons of malt. It had a crew of 19, including one woman, the cook. While working our way through a second beer we were joined by Mikhail, the first officer. Mikhail spoke little English and seemed content to watch the encounter unfold. I wondered at first if he was KGB, for surely they would have an officer on board in a foreign port. But he didn't seem the type, and I later gave up on that idea. Mikhail was 39, married with no children, and seemed captivated by us, "the Americans." Jan and the first mate were both Estonians, and though they never criticized their overlords, we were gently reminded if we accidentally referred to them as Russians.

After Mikhail joined us Jan insisted that we have champagne to toast our new friendship. We did, and then we had a second bottle. By this time we were well into a conversation that would go on for hours. From champagne we moved on to vodka (a must), then to wine, then beer (with an excellent lunch of pork chops, potatoes, and green salad), then, blessed relief, coffee with dessert; then a ship's tour—from wheelhouse to spotless engine room—then back to the dining room for more drinks and food, and more conversation. We tried several times to depart, but our hosts encouraged us to stay for the next meal or the next little cognac or the next story. And so we did.

We talked about everything, from U.S.–Russia relations and the fear of nuclear war to Alexander Solzhenitsyn and Richard Nixon. They admitted "some" Estonians might want to be free of the USSR. We discussed women's rights and raising children. We shared family photos and passports. They were shocked when we said we had only a black & white TV. We told them about our trip; they told us how the merchant marine service worked. Jan asked about wages in the U.S. and said he earned "about 500 rubles" per month (most workers earned between 100 and 150 rubles). Nothing, it seemed, was off the table, and when I infrequently rose above my alcohol-induced fog I was astounded at where we were and what we were doing—and by the apparent openness of our hosts. We laughed. Occasionally we argued a point, but it was always friendly arguing.

Of course everything they said could have been half-truths or fiction, but it didn't feel that way. It felt like an honest gab-fest between friends, accompanied by a glut of food and nonstop drinking. Thirty-six years later I can confirm that I've never drunk so much in one day, nor had such a conversation. During this long period Jennifer, with the captain's permission, wandered freely, talking to the sailors (some of whom spoke English), drifting into the captain's quarters for more pineapple juice—she avoided it for years after—and candy, which he continually urged on her despite my pleas. She joined us for meals and the tour of the ship, but spent most of her time on deck playing a mechanical hockey game with the sailors. Occasionally Ray or I would stumble from the table to check on her and she was always fine, though a little bored.

Seven-and-a-half hours after Ray had walked down the pier to say hello, after a wonderful dinner and more dessert and more cognac, and after exchanging addresses and taking photographs and saying our final goodbyes, Jan and Mikhail steered us down the steel gangplank and poured us into our faithful bus.

And I very, very carefully drove us back to the campground. Fortunately for all, it was Sunday evening in an area with little traffic, and our campsite was quite close. We made it safely home and were soon tucked in for the night. The next morning I found I had parked on a corner of the tent.

It is now six weeks since our visit to the ship in Horsens, and since Jan insisted we telephone when we got to Tallinn, I'm about to do so. We search out a public phone and I dial the number.

"Hello?" says a woman's voice. I introduce myself and ask if Jan is home. It's difficult for me to understand Russian on the phone so I don't get all she says, but this much is clear: "He is not here, it's not possible to talk. Please don't call again."

Although this is what we expected, we are disappointed.

We had only two nights in Tallinn, and most of our time was spent in the old town, wandering the cobbled streets and admiring the lovely old buildings, waiting while Ray took the perfect photograph. We found a shop selling Olympic souvenirs and bought posters and pins for friends at home. In the campground we talked with a Russian engineer and his daughter. He was learning English so I gave him one of our books, a play about Helen Keller. By late afternoon I was exhausted and not at all enthused about the fair with carnival rides that had set up not far from the campground. But Jennifer wanted to go, so Ray agreed to take her while I rested awhile.

I confess I frequently need "alone time" and hadn't had any in weeks. Thirty minutes of peace and quiet seemed like heaven; time to clean the van—as a neatnik this was an ongoing issue—and with luck to do some reading. But we had hardly pulled into the parking lot before the car was surrounded by a crowd. Ray climbed out and answered some of their questions in halting Russian and showed off the rear engine—a new concept to them. Then he and Jennifer went on to the fair, while I sat on the back seat staring out at a sea of faces.

I was dismayed, and incredibly uncomfortable; I didn't know what to do. I considered pulling the curtains, but didn't want to appear rude—they weren't staring at me, they were focused on the sink, the cupboards, the swivel seats, and the pile of belongings I was trying to sort. I hoped they would get bored and drift away, but more kept coming. After five or ten minutes I could feel my blood pressure rising, hating the situation, hating the watchers. I pulled the side curtains closed and tried to read, but curiosity simply drove them to move to the front and peer in through the windshield. At last I gave up, climbed out of the bus, slammed the door and stomped off to the carnival. After a few rides with my happy daughter I felt much better.

Looking back, I wonder why I didn't get out and talk with them, show them the interior of the bus they so longed to see. Today I'm quick to criticize that failure, and the reticence that held me back, but I also remember the exhaustion and the stress we felt—already—from being so conspicuously watched and monitored. Even Jennifer was affected. In her diary, as early as our first day in Repino, she wrote: "People STARE. You can see them poking their friends in the ribs to look. They drive me nuts!! Our car is like a zoo, too."

We were objects of blatant, unblushing curiosity wherever we went, and we just had to get used to it.

"Excuse me, please tell me, where did you buy that toilet paper?"

"Where would I buy it! These are my used ones; I'm taking them home from the dry-cleaner!"

LENINGRAD AGAIN

ON FRIDAY WE drove the 222 miles (358 kilometers) back to Leningrad and checked into the Leningrad Hotel. It was large and modern, built, we were told, by Finns, and since the balconies didn't sag and the windows all worked we agreed it must be so. It wasn't a luxurious hotel by western standards, but our room looked over the Neva River and had real beds, real toilets, and real hot water. It had been six weeks since we'd last stayed in a hotel, and we didn't care what it looked like, or even that the room was probably bugged. It felt indecently decadent, and we were definitely going to enjoy it.

But first, we desperately needed the hotel's laundry service. "*Nyet!*" said the voice on the phone, "It is not possible." So we took advantage of the hot water and washed our clothes in the bathtub. We hadn't found a laundromat in weeks and the water ran black. We wrung them out as best we could and draped them around the room to dry before going out for the day.

We headed first to the galleries of the Hermitage, one of the oldest and largest museums in the world, where we wandered from one magnificent room to the next until we could no longer absorb the beautiful, endless paintings, sculptures, and *objets d'art*. Here were paintings by Russian Masters, there were the Impressionists, ahead were the Old Masters, and still farther ahead was a sculpture gallery. From Egyptian relics to decorative arts to Renaissance paintings to post-Impressionists, every period and category of art seemed to be well represented.

From there we moved into the enormous Winter Palace stretching wide beside the Neva, through endless corridors and some of its 1,500 rooms. We admired the polished blue granite and gold trimmed paneling of the famous Jordan Staircase and were wowed by the ballrooms and magnificent halls with their massive columns; some of the state rooms could hold 10,000 people. Looking at it all, beautiful though it was, made us feel the revolution had been long overdue.

That evening we attended a folk music concert with balalaika music and wonderful dancers; a typical tourist presentation, but fun and enjoyable. When we left the hall it was pouring rain and we were in trouble. We'd been warned in Repino to remove our windshield wiper blades or they would surely be stolen. It seemed an odd thing to have to worry about, but automobile parts were almost impossible to get, so we had dutifully removed them. It was funny seeing all those drivers rushing in the rain to return their wiper blades to their rightful place, but not so funny when we found we'd left ours in the hotel room. Why? I've no idea.

Nor do I know why the Russians drove at night using only their parking lights. Whenever we tried turning on our headlights they would blink madly back at us; you could almost hear the insults. So with heavy rain spattering and streaking our windshield, we had no choice but to aim the van in the direction of the hotel, our parking lights feebly piercing the wet and dark of unknown streets. Naturally, we got lost.

The next morning, a Sunday, we woke to see the Neva River lined with flags and crowded with naval ships, including three submarines, a destroyer, and many smaller vessels. The streets were filled with throngs of people. We went out to join them, stood in line at a vendor's cart for delicious honey ice cream, and walked the riverfront with thousands of others, admiring the views and cheering the daytime fireworks, which were almost impossible to see.

Ray took dozens of photos of the river and the ships, and a young Soviet soldier—egged on by his buddies—agreed to have his picture taken with me. Looking at it now I see myself wearing a grin that hides my embarrassment, and the soldier's proud cockiness. We are standing against a granite wall with the Neva River behind us. The soldier is on my left and has angled his billed cap jauntily forward over his left eye. He's turned slightly toward me; his left hand rests confidently on his hip, his elbow jutting out. He wears a smug little smile that says, "Look at me with this capitalist woman. I am not afraid!" On my right are two men in bell-bottoms leaning against the wall, smoking. To my surprise, they totally ignore us.

After the photo was snapped we shook hands with the soldier, thanking him, and then wandered away. Since taking pictures of anything military was strictly forbidden, I was sure we'd soon be arrested.

In the afternoon we drove 25 miles east to Petrodvorets (now Petershof), built in 1714–1724 by Peter I, with its Grand Cascade fountain, gilded statues, and "jester" fountains. The huge gardens are popular with both tourists and locals. It was a hot, humid day and the shady respite was welcome. The palace wasn't open, so we drifted idly through the extensive grounds. We bypassed a large outdoor theater where a scattered audience listened to an unimpressive singer. Farther on we stood in a circle with others, listening to a blind accordion player and watching as two couples performed an informal folk dance.

Later, we watched as Jennifer joined other children searching for the hidden triggers to numerous surprise fountains, and we laughed along with the other parents when the trigger worked and the children got sprayed. We drew a few stares, but people were enjoying themselves too much to care about us. It was a relief to feel we were just one more family having a day off.

It was a casual, friendly environment with one incongruous note. The women wore dresses and even heels, and many of the men were in suits, as if they had dressed for church in a country that was rigorously atheistic. The atmosphere was relaxed, but the style was fifties formal.

The Petershof palace stands on a bluff overlooking the Gulf of Finland. It was occupied by the Nazis during the blockade of Leningrad and largely destroyed, along with most of the art—though some was hauled to Germany. This wasn't our first confrontation with the damage inflicted by the Nazis during the long siege of Leningrad in World War II. We had already visited massive St. Isaacs's Cathedral and been shown damage from bullets on the exterior walls. But on display here were photographs of the fire-gutted palace, and the comparison between post-war photos and present-day structure were striking. We were impressed with the progress of the artisanal restorers and the beauty of their work, so unlike the new construction we'd seen.

The Great Patriotic War, which is what the Soviets (our allies then) called World War II, inflicted incredible damage on the country. Approximately twenty-six million people lost their lives during the long struggle, from the German invasion on June 22, 1941, to its end on May 9, 1945. Leningrad was blockaded by the Nazis for 872 days. Hitler wanted the city razed. Estimates of casualties in that battle alone, many due to starvation, range from over one million to as many as four million. The Leningrad blockade is thought to have been the most destructive in history.

We were to see and hear evidence of the war throughout our stay; it was a scar that cut deeply across people's memories, and it remained useful as a tool of Soviet propaganda. Reminders were everywhere. Nearly every tour guide told us of the damage and loss of life their city suffered, and every town had a war memorial with an eternal flame. We saw far too many. It was traditional for newlywed couples to visit these sites and for the brides to leave their bouquets. Such traditions kept those memories alive.

That evening we had dinner at the hotel with an American journalist from Philadelphia, whose specialty was architecture. Despite living on opposite coasts and having nothing in common but our nationality, it was a relief to sit and share experiences with another American.

Before we left Leningrad we made the rounds of the hotel's public toilets looking for toilet paper, which was impossible to buy in the Soviet Union—as were feminine napkins. (I was curious to know if toilet paper was even mentioned in the government's current Five-Year Plan, but of course there was no one to ask.) The supply we brought with us was being rapidly depleted and soon we would turn to the Russian's favorite product, the newspaper *Pravda* [truth]. We were hampered in our search by the old ladies who sat inside the grand bathrooms rolling long strips of paper by hand onto individual rolls. But over the course of several trips by each of us, we were able to nab enough to carry us through to Moscow, where other deluxe hotels awaited.

Since we don't normally steal, this exercise was uncomfortable. It crossed my mind that we were very like hungry people stealing food, and my sympathy for that deed grew.

Question to Radio Armenia:
"What is the difference between a pessimist and an optimist?"

Answer:
"A pessimist is a person who says that everything around him is bad. An optimist is someone who believes that in the future nothing could be worse than it is now."

NOVGOROD

IT WAS ONLY 117 short miles (189k) from Leningrad to the city of Novgorod, where we found our small, uncomfortable campground. It was situated on a long and narrow plot of land, where dismal wooden structures—cabins of a sort—lined both sides of a strip of grass. We were directed to park our bus in a tiny empty field at the rear. High fences, a guarded gate, and loudspeakers blaring recorded music welcomed us to our next temporary home.

Like most campgrounds, this one had a cafeteria. Food being difficult to come by, we always tried at least one meal in the campground. Occasionally they were inedible; most of the time we could manage to find a dish or two that satisfied hunger. Or as I wrote in my journal, "not good, but not bad either." The utensils were aluminum, so we quickly learned to eat without jabbing an amalgam filling, which was painful. The service was generally glum.

Despite the prevailing regimentation this was the first campground not to segregate us, and we quickly found a young Russian couple to talk to. They were bicycle tourists, with a small trailer, an old canvas pup tent, and well-used 10-speed bikes. Ray's love of cycling instantly proved useful, and we enjoyed a conversation that included dedicated cycling talk and tales of their long journey. Such openness couldn't last long, however, and didn't.

"May I help you?" asked one of the camp administrators. We assured her we were doing fine, but she sat down on the grass with us anyway. Her presence quickly soured our meeting, making us all uncomfortable and turning the conversation desultory; it was clear our friendly visit had been brought to a premature end. We smiled, shook hands, and went back to the van. The next morning the cyclists were gone.

Novgorod—once known as Great Novgorod—is one of the oldest of Russian cities and one I had long wanted to see. It sits on the Volkhov River downstream from Lake Ilmen, and its history is rich in heroes and villains, including Alexander Nevsky, still one of Russia's most famous and popular leaders.

We met our guide, Marina, at 2 p.m. in front of the Intourist hotel. She was a pretty university student majoring in history and English.[13] She was eager and enthusiastic about her subject and anxious to please.

"You are my first Americans," she said proudly when we introduced ourselves. She had brought a set of matryoshka (nesting) dolls for Jennifer, with a piece of candy inside, a thoughtful gesture that immediately won over our daughter. In return we gave her a book in English, Jane Austen's *Emma*. (Our book supply decreased at a rapid rate.)

As in most small cities we used our own car, Ray driving and Marina sitting in the passenger seat pointing out the sights. Novgorod is divided by the river, with the oldest section dominated by the tall brick walls of the kremlin and the five blue and gold domes of St. Sofia's cathedral within. (Though "the Kremlin" was commonly used to represent the collective Soviet leadership, the word translates as citadel.)

Scattered throughout the town were about fifty medieval churches with their distinctive onion domes, though only one was open for services. The churches, we were told, were built by wealthy *boyars* [noblemen] to showcase their wealth as well as their faith.

Sadly, at least 30 more ancient churches were lost when Novgorod was occupied by the Nazis from 1941 to 1944. The fighting here was fierce for the two years it was on the front line. Since the fantastically domed churches were a big part of the country's charm—at least for us—we were saddened not only by the loss of so many old and beautiful buildings, but by the incredible loss of life that confronted us everywhere in Russia. Two hundred thousand people died in Novgorod; only 44 houses were left standing.

Marina took us inside two historic churches. The oldest and most important was St. Sofia's Cathedral, built in the 11th century. We strolled the grounds and explored the dark interior of the cathedral, with its beautiful frescoed walls and icons. Marina pointed to numbers painted on the backs of the old and valuable icons that hung on the intricately carved wooden iconostasis—the screen that separates the sanctuary of Orthodox churches from the nave. Apparently the Nazis had planned a heist and had numbered the icons in order to replace them correctly on the screen when they reached Berlin. Marina laughed when pointing this out. She thought the exactness very German.

As you can imagine, Germans were not well liked in Russia, even 35 years after the war. *Nemyetski*, the Russian word for German, was generally spoken as a slur, often followed by a hearty spit.

The city of Novgorod is not well known in the west. It doesn't have St. Petersburg's beauty or Moscow's political heft. But it once claimed to be something most of Russia never was—a republic.

Founded in the 9th century by a Varangian (Scandinavian) chieftain named Rurik, the city's location was ideal for trade between Byzantium in the south and northern Europe. Trade in the pelts of sable, ermine, and other fur-bearing mammals, along with timber, honey and wax, helped make Novgorod the largest city-state in medieval Europe.

Called by its residents Great Novgorod, it was a city built of wood. Excavations in the 1950s revealed 28 layers of well-preserved wooden streets, each built directly on top of the other. Using dendrochronology (tree-ring dating), it's known that the first street was laid down in 953 and the most recent in 1462. Literacy appears to have been widespread, and birch-bark books and records, as well as hoards of coins from as far away as central Asia, Persia, Syria, and Iraq help date and illuminate medieval life here.[14]

In 1136 the citizens declared Great Novgorod a republic, vesting supreme authority in a city assembly or *veche*, in which—at least theoretically—all citizens could take part. All *veche* decisions had to be unanimous, which must have made governing a slow and painful process.

Culturally and financially, the city thrived. It was Alexander Nevsky (1236–63), Russia's best-known hero, who skillfully negotiated a treaty with the Mongols that allowed the city to continue to govern itself in return for a hefty tribute. He then fought off a Swedish invasion in 1240 on the frozen Neva River (earning him the nickname Nevsky) and an attack by Teutonic Knights in 1242. The trade and crafts that were the city's *raison d'être* were obviously valued by others. And inevitably the wealthy city-state attracted the attention of the Tsars in Moscow, who were busily expanding their territory. And here another, less well known but still intriguing figure, steps forward.

Her name was Marfa Boretskaya, and in 1460 she was the wealthy widow of a former Novgorodian mayor, Isaak Andreevich Boretsky, and mother of two sons. That much is fact. The rest of her story relies on a legend that long ago captured the imagination of her countrymen and has inspired numerous plays, stories, poems, and works of art.

Briefly, the story, based on a single and probably biased source, is this: The wealthy Marfa Boretskaya was the leader of an anti-Muscovite faction that wished to maintain its trading rights and stave off annexation by Tsar Ivan III of Moscow.

Along with her two sons, Boretskaya sought help from Lithuania's Grand Duke, agreeing to hand him the city on condition that Novgorod's ancient rights be protected. (This would also drive the Orthodox church into the arms of a Catholic nation, a step considered heresy.) The negotiations failed, but news of the attempt brought Ivan into battle. He defeated Novgorod's army in 1471 and executed Marfa's son, Dmitry. Marfa continued to lead the struggle, but seven years later Ivan subjugated the city, massacred the inhabitants, and destroyed the *veche*. Marfa and her grandsons were taken into custody; her lands were confiscated, but her fate remains unknown.

A painting by Aleksey Kivshenko (1851–96) shows Marfa being escorted out of the city by guards, with the *veche* bell—the symbol of Novgorod's freedom—mounted on a sled behind her.

The tale of Marfa Boretskaya has long fascinated me, and it is still the subject of research.[15] Since many in the west—especially during the cold war—liked to assume the Russian people were incapable of self-governing, I find Marfa's story and Novgorod's long period of self-rule both revelatory and tantalizing. And I wonder if that bell is hidden away in some deep Moscow vault, or if Ivan unceremoniously destroyed it lest it ring out again.

We spent one morning driving around the small city, seeking out the old churches and taking photos. Almost all were locked, but one, isolated in a sunny green field and brilliant white under its pale blue domes, had laundry flying from lines outside—it was a blustery day—and it looked like a family or two was living there.

Farther on, a small children's park with a Ferris wheel drew our attention. It was a dreary, deserted little place where weeds struggled against hard-packed earth for a share of the sun. No children were playing. In fact, there was little play equipment except for the Ferris wheel, about thirty feet high, that stood proudly to one side. Five "buckets" held enclosed seats designed to hold up to four children. Jennifer, not surprisingly, wanted a ride. We approached the female attendant, an older woman wearing a worn blue dress, who sat hunched beside a red-trimmed metal shed. The cost was a few kopecks. She moved without words or haste to open one of the buckets, and Jennifer climbed in and sat down. The Ferris wheel began to move.

It went round and round and round. Ray and I leaned against the van, watching our daughter enjoying the ride; we agreed it was a nice find for her. And the wheel continued, round and round and round. The attendant had returned to her stool next to the shed, where she sat unmoving. We waited, expecting that any minute she would rise and bring the ride to a halt. But the wheel went round and round and round.

After about ten minutes Jennifer started fidgeting. On the downward curve she looked at us, raised her hands in a question, and rose to the top again. We shrugged our shoulders in return, thinking that her ride would surely be ending soon, and that this was really pretty funny. And the wheel went round and round. Then Jennifer began waving her arms in a frantic display. Ray walked to where the woman sat and motioned to her to end the ride. The attendant, silent and morose, rose and walked slowly to the machine; slowly, Jennifer's bucket came to a stop. She scrambled out, her face showing visible relief.

"I thought I was going to be up there *all day!*" she said.

"Well, we kept thinking she was going to stop it. But it's okay now, you're down."

"Well, if we see any more Ferris wheels, I'm *not* getting on them!"

"Okay," said Ray. "Deal."

That afternoon we drove to an outdoor museum Marina had told us about. Old log churches and a few log peasant homes (*izbas*) had been brought from all over northern Russia and rebuilt here. The museum's creators had done well, and many styles of early architecture were represented. Most appeared to have been built without nails, and the construction was impressive.

We followed paths through overgrown grass, moving from one building to another (most were locked), then tentatively climbed the steps into an open peasant *izba*. The carved wooden shutters were unpainted, but in better condition than the painted ones we sometimes spotted from the highway. Inside, the room was simply furnished with wooden benches, a table, and a large hand-painted cabinet, clearly very old. Fringed white curtains hung at the windows, and red embroidered table cloths and other handmade items were laid out for inspection. (Red is a favorite Russian color; the word's root is the same for both *red* and *beautiful*.) An old woman in a navy print dress, a white scarf tied under her chin, sat beside a large loom. We complimented her on the beauty of the work and she nodded, but didn't speak.

Outside we waded through more tall grass to a church with a high spire. A white-haired gentleman sat on a nearby log. We nodded, and he stood up and said hello in English. He was, of course, curious. Since most Russians were nervous about lengthy conversations with foreigners, especially in public places, we expected him to move on, but he stayed, and we drifted from building to building together, with him telling us about himself and Novgorod.

A mining engineer (my journal gives him no name), he was a young man of twenty when World War II started and he had volunteered, fighting in both in Novgorod and Leningrad. He was twice wounded. Saying this, he pushed back the lapel of his jacket to show us a medal.

"The war," he said, shaking his head for emphasis "was hell. Hell! But now," he said, spreading his arms, "paradise."

It was rather shocking to hear the USSR called paradise, and I had to bite my tongue. But considering what he had lived through, perhaps for him it was.

He was too young to remember the 1917 revolution, but there were some still alive who did, and when I saw very elderly people I wondered what they remembered and how they felt about it. Had they too yearned for revolution? No one denies it was warranted. Had they dreamt of utopia? Had they been good communists? Or were they opposed, indifferent? And if indifferent, did that save them?

That the revolutionary vision was distorted by madmen is not the fault of the ideas. The failure began with Vladimir Lenin, who founded the *Cheka* (secret police) as early as 1917, after which thousands of "counterrevolutionaries" were arrested, tortured, and killed. And it was Lenin who instituted censorship and took control of all newsprint. The terror birthed by him expanded exponentially under Stalin, who grabbed for power and kept it at any cost. "Power corrupts" is not an innocent aphorism.

The men and women who managed to live through the revolution and its aftermath too often found themselves in forced labor camps, suffering the horrible conditions described by Solzhenitzyn in *One Day in the Life of Ivan*

Denisovich. Most died before they saw home, and those who survived often lived out their lives in internal exile.

In 1977 the USSR was sixty years into the grand experiment. So I wondered what these old people thought of their country now. Would they agree it's paradise?

I suspected that our kind and gentle companion didn't know that when the war he had so bravely fought in ended, other Soviet soldiers—captured and kept in British or American prisoner-of-war camps—were forcibly returned home and summarily shot. Why? Because, said Stalin, they were spies. But in reality it was because they might carry home the spark of an idea.

The paradise our companion spoke of was alien to us, but we had no doubts that many of his fellow citizens would agree with him. And on this day he was no longer a soldier, but simply an engineer from Ukraine, and he was on vacation. He showed us a list of 48 Novgorod churches he hoped to photograph. One of us asked if he was a believer and he said, "No, I just like to photograph churches. I think they're beautiful."

Question to Radio Armenia:
"Why do police officers walk in threes?"

Answer:
"One knows how to read, the second knows how to write,
and the third is to keep an eye on these two members of
the intelligentsia."

KALININ

FROM NOVGOROD WE drove southeast to another old city, formerly and presently known as Tver, but in 1977 called Kalinin, after a Russian Bolshevik revolutionary. Tver, like Novgorod, was a city state until seized by Ivan III in 1485. A 16th century church is all that remains of ancient Tver, but some classical 18th and 19th century buildings offer a sense of what it once was—a frequent stopover for royalty traveling between Moscow and St. Petersburg. Kalinin was occupied by the German army in 1941, and much of it was left in ashes.

We are not in Kalinin for the history, however; it is simply the next stop on our road to Moscow, and the first campground to house us in a cabin. We have now been in the USSR twelve days and feel as though we've been here a month. But we're getting the hang of things. Days spent on the road are the easiest; we feel confident we can handle whatever comes. The cities are tougher; it's easy to get lost, and the watchfulness feels more apparent. Being constantly observed, whether by the police or people in general, remains a continuing aggravation.

When we park on a public street the bus is immediately surrounded by curious pedestrians. Just as in Tallinn, it doesn't matter that we are sitting inside. They crowd around and stare in to see what they can see. It's like being in a cage and very unpleasant, but ironic as well. As we watch and surreptitiously examine the Russians, they very openly look at us.

Often we would talk to people about the car and answer their questions. Typically, one or two men would ask Ray what kind of car it was. After this happened several times he memorized a talk in Russian, saying that it was built in West Germany, that we had bought it there new this year, and that it had an air-cooled engine. At this he would open the rear engine compartment, which inevitably led to further discussions. Once, in a village far south of Moscow, one of the onlookers insisted that the car was East German. No, Ray assured him, it was made in West Germany. They went back and forth several times and the man was so convinced Ray was lying I feared he might hit him. Such a fine vehicle, it appeared, could only have been built by Communists.

Our campground, located in a pine forest near an Intourist motel, was a pleasant surprise. The cabin, an A-shaped pale yellow building with a race car painted across the front, was roomy and clean. There were hot showers nearby and the toilets were, states my journal, "relatively clean." It was a relief after the discomfort and cramped conditions in Novgorod to be able to spread out. Our cabin looked out across a field of trees, some of which had wonderful faces carved into trunks or branches. It was clear that someone had once taken time to love this place. It was rare to see this kind of spontaneous art, and we wondered about the carver, and when and why the work had been done. It was a peaceful and quiet place, and we were grateful for the respite.

During much of our long journey we'd had rain, but now the weather was hot and humid. And just as we saw women washing clothes in ponds and streams, Ray had bathed our van near Novgorod, dipping his bucket into Lake Ilmen for water. Now we took advantage of the sun and the cabin to pull our belongings out and give everything a good airing, and the van a thorough cleaning inside.

We toured the town with a guide riding with us, but other than a collection of very old and beautiful icons my memory retains nothing whatever of Kalinen. My journal says only that we had dinner at the motel and there was a wedding party in the next room, with "a lively band."

But I do remember this about our meal: Typical of menus throughout the country, which appeared to be standardized, this one was grand in size and had page after page of elegant selections but few available items—indicated by a handwritten price. Ray and I ordered stroganoff, which we had learned was usually reliable, and Jennifer, who didn't like mushrooms, ordered an omelet—thrilled to have that choice. After a very long wait our stroganoff was delivered. After another long wait, a large and humorless woman plunked a third plate of stroganoff in front of Jennifer with a decisive, "Omelets *nyet!*" We could only laugh.

A top-level delegation of Communist party officials came to visit an asylum for the insane. In their honor, a chorus of inmates began singing the popular song "Oh, It's Great To Live In the Soviet Land."

The chairman of the delegation suddenly noticed that one man was not singing. "Why aren't you participating?" the chairman asked.

The man answered: "I'm not crazy, I'm a medic!"

MOSCOW

THERE WAS A saying in the Soviet Union that "Moscow is downhill from all the Russias." That is, the best food, goods, housing, education, jobs, and anything else you can think of, including power, settles in the capitol, leaving the regional towns and villages of the various Republics with little. We saw this pattern clearly as we drove toward and away from the city. It was also clear that the nearer one got to Moscow the more regulated, regimented, and circumspect the populace became.

In far-away Estonia people had seemed more relaxed, the regulations less onerous. One theory suggested that the central government permitted certain republics more freedom to keep them quiet and toeing the party line. That reflected what we were seeing. There were clear differences between the four republics we visited: Estonia, Russia, Georgia, and Ukraine. And in Moscow there was no mistaking who ruled.

Throughout our travels we saw banners and posters proclaiming the worker's paradise and urging citizens to be good workers, socialists, and Communists. They were everywhere. I quit reading them because I felt like I was being yelled at all the time, and my guess is no one else read them either. In Camping Butova, on the southern edge of Moscow, there were many signs, many regulations, and many people who had let power go to their heads.

The front gate was staffed with old men who, with the authority granted by their red arm bands, demanded we show our passes going in or out. No matter how many times we crossed their paths and showed our passes, they looked on us with suspicion, yelling and gesturing and exerting their authority. The campground was extremely crowded, and though we put up our tent we never used it, because each time we returned we had lost the parking space next to it, and had to find a new one. It was a frustrating stay.

We were surprised to find the city so hot and smoggy, a condition that didn't help our moods. Still, we were excited about being in Moscow. We took our guided tour with others in a rattling old bus that lacked air conditioning. We were shown all the famous sites—and there are many—but there were no stops, and our female guide kept up a steady stream of Soviet cant. Although the tour provided us with an orientation to this city of seven million, we learned very little and felt relieved when it was over.

We went back to our van and drove to Red Square, where we parked and walked until our feet hurt: across the broad, almost endless paving stones to the Kremlin to view the many onion-domed churches inside its walls, not forgetting the giant bell that fell the first time it was used and sits there still. Much of the city, including the Kremlin churches, were under repair and surrounded by scaffolding in preparation for the upcoming 1980 Olympics.

From the Kremlin we walked to the resplendent and complex, nine-domed, St. Basil's Cathedral, color rippling in the waves of heat that rose from the cobbled pavement. The cathedral was consecrated in 1561 to celebrate Muscovy's capture of Kazan, and is surely the most photographed and best-known monument in Russia.

And finally we walked into the mammoth, overheated department store, GUM (the Government Universal Magazine). We said No to Lenin's tomb, where the line stretched across the square. Seeing Lenin was never on our list.

Was all this vastness a deliberate attempt to make both visitors and citizens feel powerless and insignificant? Probably. But the Russians, I was learning, like our countrymen the Texans, want everything they own to be the biggest and the best.

Still, Moscow is a beautiful old city. From its ancient beginnings as a village beside the Moskva river, it spread in concentric circles around the old, fortified *kremlin*. From 1340 to 1712 it was the capitol of Great Russia, also called Muscovy. In 1713 Peter I moved the capital to his new city of St. Petersburg. Lenin moved it back to Moscow in 1922, where it remained. Since 1991 it has been the capitol of the Russian Federation.

Visiting GUM, where we'd hoped to buy a few gifts, was an exercise in futility. It was very hot, there was no air conditioning, and it was crowded and pungent. The Russians used no deodorants, probably because they weren't for sale. GUM was not one grand department store, but rather many small shops on several floors. We crushed our way through crowds into various stores, only to find there was nothing to buy or nothing we wanted, before moving on to the next. It wasn't long before we gave up and sought relief outside, in the hot, polluted air, our long effort winning us only a yellow hair ribbon for Jennifer. Across the square, near the Kremlin wall, was a *vada* (water) machine. We headed for it.

I have written that we occasionally found Pepsi Cola but it was rare, as were other kinds of Russian soft drinks. What we did find, especially in cities, were flavored water dispensers. These were about the size of the familiar soft drink dispensers at home. I never drank what came out of these machines, but Ray and Jennifer did. Here's what Jennifer says about them in her diary:

"First you get a glass, you clean it." [There was one communal glass, "cleaned" by placing it upside down and pushing a button that sent a small jet of water into the glass.] "Put in three kopeks or something, and surprisingly I always get what I want out of two choices. I want the brown stuff with foam that looks like '*piva*.' [beer] It tastes like lemonade. Russian lemonade. *Ochen Horasho!*" [Very Good!] And, she adds, "In Russia the *moroshnoe* [ice cream] is very good! Yum!" And it was.

(Jennifer had quickly memorized two Russian sentences: "Ice cream, please," and "I don't understand." They served her well.)

In addition to carts selling ice cream, we also found carts selling *pirogi*, pastries filled with potatoes, cheese, onions, or meat, for eight kopeks each. Two of them made a filling lunch, and when we found them we bought them. They were cheap, tasty and easy; we refused to think about what we might be eating.

After our experience at GUM we gave in and went to the *Beriozka* in one of Moscow's largest hotels. *Beriozkas* were stores that stocked all manner of goods, imported and domestic. Russians with influence (*blat*), or those who were lucky enough to travel or work abroad (which also produced *blat* in the form of foreign currency), could shop at such stores, which were usually hidden away on side streets. The best of the best could be bought in the shops that catered to people such as government leaders, influential writers, performers, and athletes. More openly, there were small shops that catered to tourists in the hotels and accepted only foreign currency. They stocked typical tourist items like fur hats and caviar, matryoshka dolls and other souvenirs, and imported alcohol and cigarettes.

We generally avoided these shops—their exclusionary practice made us uncomfortable—but inevitably, with our limited time and growing frustration, we ended up shopping there. Unfortunately they didn't sell groceries. On this occasion we were after some good chocolate to lift our spirits, a few gifts to take home, and several packs of Camel cigarettes to give as gifts. (Older Russian men fondly remembered Camels from the war and were always happy to receive them.) When we walked in, it was apparent that something was amiss.

A well-dressed American man was standing at the counter speaking loudly to a female employee who was clearly unhappy.

"You're nasty, you're just nasty," he said loudly. "I want to know why you're so nasty. You're not good for this shop, and you're not good for the Soviet people."

Did he really think this was helping his case?

"I want to see your manager," he said then. "I want to speak to whoever's in charge!"

"It is not possible" said she, grimly. Another young woman, also an employee, wandered over to stand beside the first in support.

"Don't you people know the meaning of service?" said the American, his voice rising.

We wanted to tell him he was wasting his time, but that would have been wasting ours. He was a disappointing stereotype: arrogant, demanding, and determined to pound into the heads of these two young women the American concept of service—which meant squat to the two girls. They were guaranteed a job whatever happened. As long as they showed up and put in their time, they got paid. And they cared not what the customer thought.

I admit I was sympathetic to the girls, despite their sullen and unfriendly attitude. But who could blame them? No one likes being yelled at, even when the words aren't understood.

Embarrassed by our countryman, we quickly stepped to the second counter and paid for our purchases. I wanted to say, "We're not all like him," but it was pointless; they didn't care what we thought either. Meanwhile, the angry customer, ignored by the two women, made his way to the door and, walking out, said loudly, "I'm going to complain to your supervisor! You'll hear about this!"

Complaints like this never sound original; they are as cardboard-cutout as the people who speak them.

We were heading for the door when the two women began shooing the remaining few customers out of the shop, flapping their hands and saying "goodbye, goodbye" in broken English. As we stepped onto the street they slammed the door, pulled down the shade, and put up a "Closed" sign.

So much for teaching good service.

We come now to the visit mentioned at the beginning of this book, our meeting in Moscow with Ilya and Elena. It was a planned encounter, the lucky or serendipitous result of a young Russian woman, Tanya, being assigned as a teaching assistant to Dr. B. She arrived in the classroom about a month before we were due to leave on our trip, and I asked her advice. She willingly gave us tips on what to see in Moscow, but like most Russians, she hadn't traveled much beyond her home. A few weeks after our first conversation she stopped me after class and asked the big question: would we be willing to take a few gifts to her mother, Elena, and stepfather?

(Tanya's father was Jewish and had emigrated to the U.S. She was later given permission to join him and did so knowing she might never see her mother again.)

I said yes, of course, while wondering how we could fit more into our already filled duffle bags. When the time came I met her for coffee and she handed over a shopping bag full of clothing, cosmetics, and other incidentals. I groaned inwardly, it was more than I'd expected.

Tanya had written to her mother and now gave me explicit instructions. I was to memorize her mother's phone number ("Do not write it down anywhere!"), go to a public booth in Moscow after dark, and when the phone was answered say only, *"Ya ot Tani"* (literally, I am from Tanya). Her mother or stepfather would then give me instructions about where to meet.

It sounded melodramatic, but since it was risky for Soviet citizens to fraternize with foreigners neither she nor her mother, nor we, were willing to take chances. Even in the van we carefully mixed her gifts with our belongings so as not to appear suspicious. I worried that the border guards might question several pairs of new, unworn jeans because they were obviously salable, but like the rest of our clothes they were ignored.

We left Camping Butova after dinner the evening of our first day in Moscow and I nervously placed the call. We were to meet Elena in front of the main PTT (Post, Telegraph, Telephone office) at high noon the following day. Meanwhile, we had earlier been approached by a female official in the campground, who was both pleasant and spoke excellent English. Since most Russian officials weren't pleasant, she was, we thought, a little too smooth, and we suspected she was KGB. Our conversation had been general; she asked about our trip, wished us a happy stay in Moscow, and left.

The next morning we drove into Moscow, this time with Tanya's gifts in two plastic bags. We were naturally anxious, wondering what the day would bring.

We parked a few blocks from our destination and walked to the PTT. As in most Russian cities the sidewalks were jammed with people; few had cars and most used the trams or the beautiful and excellent subway, and walked. At the PTT main entrance we pushed through the crowd and climbed to a spot near the top of the steps where we turned and stood, looking for an unknown woman in a crowd of unknowns. It was five minutes to noon.

And from out of the crowd stepped the same female campground official, smiling and greeting us by name with a friendly hello.

We were shocked. What the hell was she doing here? Could they have traced the phone call? Or did she follow us here? Would this mean problems for Elena? We fought panic to greet her casually.

"What are you doing here?" she asked, smiling.

"Meeting a friend," said Ray. Best to be honest. And at that moment up strode a well-dressed blond woman.

"Mr. and Mrs. Gilden?" she asked in heavily accented English.

"Yes, hello!" I said, stupidly waving my hand while thinking, egad, what now?

Ray quickly introduced the two women and they stood on the steps below us and held a brief conversation; much too quick and quiet for me to comprehend. Then the campground official smiled, wished us a good visit and disappeared into the crowd. Elena said quickly in Russian, "Let's get a taxi."

"We'll follow you," I replied.

Ray and I looked at each other, our eyes sharing the same question. What brought the official from the campground, and should we still go with Elena? I had no doubt it was Elena, but what if it wasn't? He picked up the bags, I took Jennifer's hand, and we followed the stranger down the street.

The taxi took us across town and through block after depressing block of gray high-rise apartment buildings. We'd had a brief exchange of small talk, but Elena was either not willing to speak in the taxi or unsure of her English and my Russian. The day, as yesterday, was hot, the air humid and smog-filled, the taxi cramped. The long ride was essentially silent. About the time I was beginning to wonder if we had been kidnapped, Elena signaled the driver to park at a high-rise entrance. Thirty or forty minutes after we'd climbed in, we climbed out, relieved to be at our destination.

"Here we go," I thought as we squeezed into the tiny, dirty elevator.

It was a relief when Elena unlocked her door and invited us in to their small, modern apartment. Her husband Ilya met us at the door with a welcome smile on his face.

"Come in!" he said in perfect English.

Ilya is polite, gentlemanly, intense. They overwhelm us with hospitality, genuinely concerned for our comfort. It is so hot; they are sorry about the heat. Would we like to take showers? A nap? No? Then perhaps a cool drink, some tea? A lemonade? A vodka? We laugh at that, and accept tea.

And Ilya reaches over and unplugs the phone. "Maybe listeners," he says.

We ask about the meeting at the PTT, explaining that we were surprised the woman from the campground had appeared at exactly the right time. Ilya translates our comments to Elena and then reassures us. "Don't worry about it," he says.

Ilya is a translator for *Literaturnaya Gazeta,* a weekly, influential newspaper, and is anxious to discuss American idioms he doesn't understand, though his English is excellent. He shows us a censored copy of *Newsweek* with empty squares where articles once hung, articles he is not allowed to know about. He is disgusted with the censoring, but he values his job. He points to an article he is working on.

"What does this mean?" he asks: "Spare the rod and spoil the child."

Elena, in the meantime, has arranged an elegant lunch: salads, cheeses, fresh fruit, even caviar. We express surprise at the variety, for finding good food has become an obsession with us, and she explains that because she is a doctor and has access to many people she can trade her services for food and small luxuries. She shows us a red notebook filled with names she can call on for wanted items. The caviar came from one, the tomatoes from another.

It is all illegal, of course, this underground economy, but it is as natural to the Soviets as breathing.

As we sit down to lunch they are full of questions. About Elena's daughter Tanya; and about America itself. Can we please explain the contradictions Ilya sees in his reading? Can we clarify the truth of what they are hearing from others, or what he has read in his half-mutilated publications? We try to supply answers, but we are almost as ignorant of current events as they. For months we've been traveling with no radio and no skills for the reading of foreign newspapers. But it doesn't matter, really. They want to know everything. They don't care if we talk about our home in Oregon, life in the U.S., or what we've seen on the road. They would, if they could, suck the thoughts right out of our heads, they are so hungry for news and truth.

And so we decide to go out, to a park they know where it is safer to talk, where potential listeners are more obvious. But first they must give us a gift. Elena excuses herself and leaves the room, coming back with a small hand-loomed rug. "It's from Moldavia," she says. "We hope you like it." We do. We still have it.

"And, now, before we go," says Ilya, "we would like to ask a favor."

"Of course," I say.

"Well, it's a big favor, so don't be too quick." Elena holds out her hand and shows us a solitaire diamond ring.

"This was Tanya's," Ilya tells us. "When we took her to the airport to fly to America, she was about to board when one of the soldiers grabbed her hand and removed it. He said, 'You cannot take this, it belongs in Russia. And you will never see your homeland again.' It was very upsetting for her. Will you take this ring to Tanya?"

I look at Elena. "Please," she says.

I look at Ray. He says, "We're only hesitating because when we entered the country we had to sign a pledge stating that we had no subversive books, drugs, a long list of items. And one of those was diamonds. But yes, we'll take it to her."

"But you must not risk your safety," says Ilya.

"It's all right," says Ray, and I agree. "We can find a way to hide it."

After we reassure them once more Ilya hands me the ring. I carefully put it in a zipper pocket of my purse. And we go out for our walk.

So here we are, friends strolling the gravel paths, wandering the grounds of a pre-revolutionary mansion on a hot and smoggy day. That we are friends is not doubted. That ineffable understanding—empathy, attachment, whatever it is that defines friendship, has rooted. The other, the unknown, the enemy, is routed.

It is our turn to ask questions now, about their culture, about how things work, about the dissident movement and the underground writings known as *samizdat*. And then the practical questions like finding vegetable markets and how to act when we're approached by the KGB. They suggest places for us to visit in Moscow and I ask about getting to Zagorsk, a nearby city full of beautiful Russian architecture that we are not permitted to visit.

And then Ilya, walking ahead of us, suddenly turns back and asks the oft-asked question: "But tell us about this wonderful trip of yours, how is it possible that you can do this, that you can come *here* even?" And we halt on the path, laughing because we've had to explain this so often during our journey, and I say, "Oh well, you know, it was just an idea. . . ."

"Oh," he says. And after a pause, "You know, we too can have thousands of ideas. But they all die within us."

It's difficult to describe the impact that simple statement had upon us. It echoed throughout the remainder of our trip, through all the many conversations we had with Russians, Ukrainians, Georgians, Romanians, Yugoslavs. And long after we were home and busy with our lives; years after all the slide shows and talks and questions were done with; decades after the trip itself, it was that single episode we spoke of when people asked us about traveling in the Soviet Union. "We too can have thousands of ideas, but they all die within us." That line is burned into my soul.

And because we knew it was true, there was little more to say. Our two worlds had briefly merged, but this was a divide we were powerless to transcend. The five of us slowly retreated up the pebbled path while the heat and smog pressed down and uneasiness returned. We exited the grounds of the old mansion and walked together, making small talk, to a nearby metro station. We asked if we could write when we got home, perhaps send them something. But they said no, they already heard from Tanya and if they got too many letters from foreigners, well . . . the sentence tailed off.

Ilya and Elena helped us find the right train, then we hugged them both in turn and climbed aboard. And they stood on the platform and waved goodbye as the train began to move.

We never saw or heard from them again.

Throughout our trip we sought out places and events that Jennifer would enjoy too, and the famous Moscow circus was one of those. We went that evening and found ourselves seated among other Americans, people who were visiting Moscow with a tour group.[16] We all loved the circus. The performances were wonderful, the color and lights and excitement were everything you could wish for in a circus. But almost more entertaining—at least for Ray and me—were the reactions we got from our seat mates when in response to their questions we admitted we weren't traveling with a group but on our own and without a guide. You could see our remarks being passed down through the group; it was like watching an extended game of Gossip. Their comments came back to us the same way: astonishment, shock, curiosity. We were brave, we were foolish, they didn't know it was possible, they wouldn't have dared. And then the questions: were we afraid? followed? how long was our trip? where were we going? what did we think?

In truth the group was seeing places and events we didn't have an opportunity to see—either because our travel schedule was too tight or because we didn't know about them, or we couldn't get tickets or they were too expensive, or they simply weren't open to independent travelers. But despite those negatives, and despite envying them their comfortable four-star hotels, we knew we were happier traveling the way we were. We were learning about the Soviet Union in a far different way than our compatriots, and we believed we were getting more for our money. It was then that we adopted the words that would become our lifelong mantra: "The cheaper the trip the richer the experience." We've used it so often it's trademarked.

One more incident marked our stay in Moscow. It happened the morning we were scheduled to leave the city. We were running short of petrol coupons, which could only be purchased with dollars. Usually we bought them at campgrounds, but in this case they were locked in the campground safe and no one had the key. We had to drive across the city to the Ukraine Hotel, housed in one of Stalin's neo-Gothic towers. By this time we had been in the country long enough to be increasingly irritated by the red tape and constant demands of campground officials and others.

And we weren't happy about having to drive miles across the city when we had a long drive ahead of us. At any rate, I was ready to lose my temper, and did. Later I thought it was comical and copied the conversation into my journal. To appreciate this you must remember that we were on a $25-a-day budget and that a dollar in 1977 wasn't just change. (A U.S. gallon of gas cost 62 cents and the median U.S. home price was $38,500.)

I stood in line for the teller—who, like most Russian clerks, was unsmiling and sullen. When my turn came I asked for and received the necessary coupons and paid for them. Then she said, "One dollar."

"What for?"

"One dollar."

So I begrudgingly gave her four quarters. She examined them all carefully and then, apparently because one was a bicentennial quarter (1976) and therefore different, she took them to the next teller and they both examined them, turning them over and endlessly comparing one to another while holding a whispered conversation. This took more than five minutes and I was beginning to boil. Then she came back and laid them all on the counter, shoving the bicentennial towards me. She pointed at it, meaning they wouldn't accept it.

"One dollar," she said again.

"No," I said. Then, counting loudly, I touched each quarter stating, "Twenty-five, fifty, seventy-five, one dollar."

The second clerk, who spoke English, stepped up.

"We must have paper dollar," she said.

"That is all I have," said I in Russian.

"Then you must go to the *Beriozka* shop." I felt like saying, "You go to the *Beriozka* shop!"

The man behind me in line was getting restless.

"But what's it for?" I asked.

"What?"

"What am I paying for? What's the dollar *for*?" I was getting loud, turning into the ugly American.

"Just a minute," said clerk number two, who then walked away.

Clerk number one proceeded to write a receipt, still eyeing suspiciously the strange metal disk she'd decided to keep to get rid of me. She shoved the receipt toward me; I grabbed it and stomped off, happy that I hadn't had to traipse to the *Beriozka* and waste more precious time.

It was a small victory, but one that left me identifying with the Russians, who daily confronted, and won or lost at the hands of the omnipresent, complex, strangely unrealistic, and unpredictable bureaucracy. It felt good to win.

My journal entry ends with "That's the way Moscow seemed to me, full of frustration; oppressive, watchful. We were happy to leave the city and start for Oryol, even though we'd heard nothing but bad about that campground."

The Russians presented us with two faces. When meeting them privately, in conversations in the campgrounds or wherever they felt safe, they were warm, friendly, sentimental, generous, humane. But when acting in an official capacity—at any level—they could be cold, rude, grim, unsmiling, and rigid. Even the old *babushkas* who worked as key ladies in the hotels liked to order guests around. But standing up for ourselves—as the French woman had when border guards wanted to slash her seats—caused confusion, and the workers, the bureaucrats, would retreat, just as the hotel teller had. We would use that tactic again.

In his book, *The Russians,* a wonderfully detailed and intimate portrayal of Soviet life in the early 70s, Hedrick Smith had this to say in his chapter about the public/private split that we saw so frequently. Here he is writing specifically about the children of the well-educated, or "intelligentsia," but I suspect the same could be said of nearly all Soviet families, especially those living in cities.

"More typically, several intellectual families privately told us, children learn quite early in life about the schizophrenic split between talking freely at home but carefully conforming and concealing their views in public. . . . 'Maybe no one tells children specifically not to speak out, [said one father] but they are canny and they learn the cynicism from their parents.'" [17]

This split became more obvious the longer we were in the country. Russians showed a blank, often dispirited face in public—a face designed to draw little or no attention. Often for good reason. For just as Elena worked the system by privately treating patients, so did they all. Everyone had an angle, a way to get more of whatever it was they needed—and they were good at it. They bought and sold under the table. They traded goods for services. They did favors. They speculated. They stole and resold government property. It was all done *nalevo*, "on the left." Everyone did it and everyone ignored the doing, because to admit it—to even draw attention to it—was inconceivable. The only way for the country to avoid disaster was to ignore what everyone knew.

I thought then that if Russians suddenly found themselves living anywhere outside the USSR, they would surely be successful, because they knew instinctively how to find the cracks in a system, how to make the weakness work to their advantage. And maybe that explains the rapid growth and success of the Russian mafia. They were already living dual lives corrupted by secrecy and greed; when all control collapsed they just took it to a higher level.

Leningrad ice cream line.

Jennifer uses her
Russian to say, "Ice
cream please."

Navy Day on the Neva River

A typical driving day. We follow trucks while Jennifer reads. Note the missing wiper blades, removed to prevent theft.

Old Tallinn skyline.

Our Novgorod friend shows off his pin commemorating the 25th anniversary of the end of the Great Patriotic War (WWII).

Above: A wooden church at the outdoor museum. *Left*: Church of SS Peter and Paul, Novgorod (1406)

The wealth of the Tsars is reflected in these two photos. *Above*, Petrodvorets (Petershof), after its restoration. The building was gutted and the fountains destroyed during WWII.

Below, the famous Jordan staircase in the Winter Palace in Leningrad.

Lenin overlooks the highway
to the Caucasus Mountains

The van was always a
source of curiosity and
often drew a crowd.

Above: A woman does laundry as her family looks on. Such scenes were a common sight along the road.

Below: It surprised us to see horse carts still being used.

The winding road through the Caucasus Mountains.

Below: Women selling fruit along the roadside. Such markets were rare and we were always happy to find them.

107

Red Square, with GUM on the left, St. Basil's center, and Lenin's tomb and the Kremlin walls on the right.

Jennifer waits while Ray drinks flavored water from a *Voda* machine.

Visitors at the Moscow eternal flame honoring war dead of WWII.

Ivan the Great bell tower, Moscow

Karen being weighed in Tbilisi.

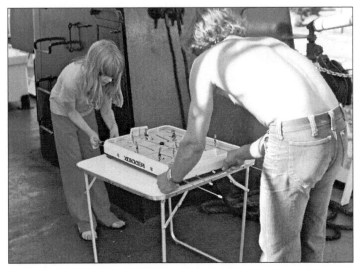

Jennifer plays hockey with a sailor on board the Russian freighter in Horsens.

Mixed crew of railroad workers

110

The Kursk War Memorial. The "greatest tank battle in history" commenced July 12, 1943 and was a turning point of the war.

A soldier takes a picture at Lenin's tomb in Moscow.

A trial. The sentence: ten years exile to Solovky.
"And just where is Solovky?" asked the convicted man.
"In the far north."
"Under whose authority?"
"Soviet, of course!"
"Then couldn't you send me somewhere farther?"

POSTCARDS FROM THE ROAD

FROM MOSCOW TO Oryol, from Oryol to Kursk, from Kursk to Kharkov, the road took us farther from Moscow and the center of power, and deep into Russian farmland. Our long days on the road turned into a kind of meditation; navigating the narrow, bumpy highways, looking out at the endless rolling farmland and observing life in the villages we passed, where women washed clothes in ponds or streams and pulled water from village wells; where outhouses were common while television antennas sprouted from roofs, disseminating the party line. It was clear that Lenin's efforts to electrify the countryside had mostly succeeded. It was a shame he hadn't also provided plumbing.

Ray did most of the driving and I spelled him. Jennifer sometimes read for hours, powering her way through the *Lord of The Rings* trilogy. We followed the underpowered and slow trucks that were often filled to overflowing with building supplies or other goods. Bits and pieces periodically fell off, to be immediately picked up by the next car following.

I remember especially a truck loaded with bricks. But the bricks weren't on pallets, as one would expect. They were simply thrown in, helter-skelter, and of course many were broken. We followed this truck several miles, until it turned off to the right. And looking out my side window, I could see a large building in progress, with heaping piles of bricks spread across the building site. The one closest to me had tire tracks across it, the bricks crushed. It was Ilya who told us "building begins and ends in vodka," and I wondered if that was the problem here. Or was it simply that no one cared?

In Vladimir Bukovsky's amazing book *To Build a Castle—My Life as a Dissident,* he tells of working in a bus factory where "my classmates and I saw for the first time what a Soviet enterprise is like—with all its deceptions, its hollow façade, and its coercion. Nobody in the bus factory was in a hurry to work . . . In the mornings they were almost all drunk or hung over . . . They stole practically anything that could be sold on the black market or used at home. One day they stole a whole bus engine, another a roll of material for upholstering the seats."[18]

South of Moscow we passed what looked like an unfinished factory standing in a weedy field. Its rusted iron beams crossed and recrossed, enclosing multiple stories of empty air. Ray thought it would make an interesting photo, so he pulled off the road and dug out his camera. A minute after he snapped the picture a motorcycle policeman with an automatic rifle on his back pulled up behind us.

I quickly pulled out a map and as he approached the window we pretended to be studying it.

"It is not possible to stop here!" he said, after closely examining Ray's I.D.

"We're just looking to see where the next petrol station is," I said. "Can you . . .?

"It is not possible to stop here!"

"Okay, we're going," Ray said. And we went.

In Oryol we met an Italian couple from Sardinia who were also traveling in a VW van. They were having engine problems, and Ray offered to help. The wife had also studied Russian for two years and we had a lot in common, so it was a fun and light-hearted evening until a young Russian man joined us. We had been told by other campers we might be approached by KGB in the Oryol campground, so we were wary when he told us he was a student who wanted to try out his English. He hung around for an hour, following us back to the van, repeating that he wanted to give us a tour of Oryol the next day. We declined his offer and he left reluctantly.

These approaches always followed the same pattern. Sometimes there would be one young man, sometimes two. Always neatly dressed, they "just wanted to talk" and to give us a tour of their city, but they were stiff and unnatural and overly persistent, and their conversations were predictable.

Whether they were actual KGB or KGB in training, or just students with a summer job keeping an eye on the foreign tourists, they were doing a lousy job, and we always found them annoying. And obvious.

Russians were great readers, and most received an adequate education, though the curriculum was standardized across the nation and individualism was punished. Getting into a university was highly competitive, and fields of study had to be chosen before one ever crossed a university threshold. Students who completed courses and graduated were guaranteed a job in their chosen field, though often in a place not of their choosing.

In a campground far south of Moscow we talked to a teacher of English in a country school who complained the children didn't want to learn. "All they're interested in is tractors," he said. I doubt that teacher chose his location, but he chose his vocation and there he was.

Along the highway outside of Kursk, 280 miles south of Moscow, is a war memorial. We had seen many memorials, but this one was different. It marked the site of the largest tank battle ever held—and a turning point in World War II. It was here, in July, 1943 that the Soviet army, our ally in that conflict, halted the German blitzkrieg. Almost a million men (Soviets and Germans) were killed or injured during the multiple battles around Kursk.

The monument was impressive; I remember walking down a short flight of stairs into a kind of tunnel where photographs of the battle were displayed and solemn music played. In front, an eternal flame burned in the center of a large paved plaza, and red tulips bloomed beside a mounted tank. After visiting so many sites in Russia where the Nazis had prevailed, it felt good to cheer the Red Army's win in this crucial battle. We discovered we were partisans after all.

Breaking up our long days on the road were stops for petrol. We tried to get this done early in the morning because it usually meant, on average, a two-hour wait in line. But we often didn't have a choice since stations were separated by long distances. Sometimes other people, seeing our foreign car, or maybe the USA (in Russian) on our dash or in the back window, would move us to the front of the line. Once or twice a policeman moved us, and at least once the station operator did. We didn't like the preferential treatment, preferring to experience things the way the Soviets did. But being moved ahead was a great benefit, since we usually had eight-to-ten-hour drives between our assigned destinations, and no permission to overnight elsewhere.

Ray had been wanting a photo of the long petrol lines so one morning he opened the car door, climbed out and took one. This considerably upset the man in front of us, and he said something to Ray that I couldn't hear, but I could tell it wasn't pleasant.

About ten minutes later a second driver brazenly cut in front of us. Most people were waiting outside their vehicles, and when they saw this they started yelling at him. He ignored them and us. However, after he got his gas and had been inside to pay, he turned around and hollered at us before climbing into his car. We weren't sure whether he was angry about the photograph or because we were Americans, but it upset us, and we had a hard time shaking it.

Such incidents were rare. Most people, in fact, went out of their way to help us when they could. In my journal, after reporting this I wrote, "Russians are so volatile and un-predictable. There is definitely a touch of anarchy in them."

A big benefit of traveling south of Moscow was that we were able to find more fresh food. Our first indication was a peasant woman—easily identified by her sack-like print dress and a headscarf—standing beside the road with a bucket of potatoes. Ray braked immediately and I got out. I quickly learned I was expected to buy the entire bucket, but we had no room to store them. After a bit of bargaining I convinced her to sell me just a few. Through that day and the next we saw more women selling potatoes, and soon it was tomatoes and more. South of Kharkov we came upon our first real veg-gie and fruit stand with several peasant women selling their produce. And they had scales! This was underlined in my journal, so it must have been a great leap forward. We bought pears, tomatoes, a pepper, and sunflower seeds. Across the street a stand was selling fresh rolls and sweet breads, so we bought some of those too. It felt like Christmas.

Jennifer had gone off to find ice cream, and when I found her she was talking and trading pins [19] with three little girls. It was a pleasant stop and lifted our spirits after the morning's confrontation.

I was still at the bread stand when the seller asked the question I had been dreading. She was a typical peasant, dressed in a well-worn flowered house dress, her hair covered by a white scarf. Her faced was deeply lined, her hands well calloused. She stood inside, her brown, muscled arms resting on the window sill of the wooden booth. Her bread and rolls were stacked high on rough boards behind her, and the inviting scent of fresh bread drifted through the window.

Not surprisingly, she asked where I was from. I must add that it was impossible to hide our foreignness or try to look like Russians. Even if we had purchased Russian clothes we would have stood out. As Dr. B. was fond of saying, "Americans just look different. They walk differently, they move differently. You'll never fool anyone by just changing your clothes." We didn't try.

She asked me where I was from.

"America," I said. (I had given up saying the United States. To everyone we are Americans.)

"Ah," she said with a big smile, "how do you like our country?"

"Very much! It's beautiful here," I said.

"And which do you think is better," said she, "America or the Soviet Union?"

Oh crap, I thought. Should I lie and make her happy? Or I should I be honest?

"Hmm," I hesitated, then said, "America." Her face immediately fell; her eyes shuttered. I felt awful. But after a moment the shade lifted and she gave me a half-smile and nodded.

"Well, I think it is natural," she said. "You like your country best and I like mine."

"Yes," I agreed with a smile. "It's natural."

She handed over the rolls, and we shook hands and I walked slowly back to the van, wondering. If I had said, "the Soviet Union is better" would she have believed me? I think she would.

Despite its large collective and cooperative state farms, the Soviet Union could not feed its people without the produce grown on private plots of land (one-half acre under Khruschev, but increased to one acre by Breshnev) and brought to the cities by individual farmers, like the women at that local stand. There were vast differences between the poor land of central Russia, plagued by icy winters and thaws that oozed thick mud for months, and the rich earth and plentiful sun of south Ukraine, Georgia, and the southeast republics. The Russian peasants appeared poor and visibly worn down by their hard lives. Their harvest of potatoes and other cold-friendly crops brought little money compared to the variety of vegetables, fruit, and even flowers grown in the south. Hedrick Smith, in *The Russians*, offers this about the production of food in the USSR:

"The private plots that produce these goods are small and mostly farmed part-time but the volume of their output is so enormous and essential to the Soviet economy that the nation's 250 million people could not be fed without it."

Then he quotes an "unusual article" from March 1975 that "revealed that 27 percent of the total value of Soviet farm output—about $32.5 billion worth a year—comes from private plots that occupy less than one percent of the nation's agricultural lands (about 26 million acres). [20]

It's beyond the scope of this book and this author to explain the Soviet economy. But it is important to know that the split between the people lucky enough to live in cities, and the grueling, almost inhuman existence of the poorest of peasants ran counter to both Soviet socialist doctrine and the glowing paeans to workers one saw and heard throughout the country. And if you were a peasant farm worker you had little hope of improving your life. In 1977 many still had no internal passports, meaning they could not travel easily or leave their home village and move to a nearby town, let alone a city like Moscow or Leningrad. They were almost as tied to the land as they had been when Tolstoy was writing about the serfs. In fact, there wasn't much that separated them. The village students who were interested not in English but in tractors may have had a good reason. Tractor and other machine drivers worked less and earned more money than field hands.

Sometimes during our long drives I thought about the people we would never meet, the ones imprisoned or sent to labor camps for writing or speaking what they thought—or for painting unacceptable subjects or in a style not deemed worthy of Soviet art. There were hundreds of thousands; no one knew for sure. And if prison and labor camps weren't bad enough, dissidents could also find themselves in the

Serbsky Institute of Forensic Psychiatry or other mental hospitals, where the staff included KGB. These prisoners were pronounced insane and "treated" with drugs indefinitely simply because they spoke out against the system. Vladimir Bukovsky, who spent time at Serbsky, in labor camps, and in various prisons simply for expressing his ideas, wasn't anticipating the current self-publishing wave when he wrote, "I would erect a monument to the typewriter too. It brought forth a new form of publishing, *samizdat*, or 'self-publishing': write myself, edit myself, censor myself, publish myself, distribute myself, go to jail for it myself." [21]

Our campgrounds varied, but were uniformly bad when it came to toilet facilities. In Kharkov I remember only two women's toilets in the campground. They were the "squat" variety and sat inside stalls in a small wooden building. They had not been cleaned in a long time. Two sinks hung on a side wall. The entire facility was filthy, with muddy floors and grimy wood walls. These "restrooms" smelled so bad that both Jennifer and I took a deep breath and held it before diving in to use them. But Russian women and children were standing inside chatting, using the washbasins and leisurely combing their hair. We could hardly bear to breathe, but they seemed immune to it all.

And there were no roadside rest stops. We joked about seeing tufts of white paper scattered through the fields, but out of necessity we added to that litter ourselves. At least we knew where not to step. Even when gas stations had toilet facilities they were usually outhouses that you could smell before you got close. I remember opening the door to one to see a mound of feces completely covering the porcelain footprints one was expected to stand on.

Somewhere south of Moscow Ray began experiencing signs of dysentery, which made road travel even less appealing for him. Fortunately, we had hit up the Moscow hotels for toilet paper and had a reasonable supply. Also fortunately, neither Jennifer nor I seemed to have it.

One day we were driving down a lonely section of highway and spotted a pretty church tower in a village, maybe a half mile off the main road.

"Let's go over there," I said, "I want to see that church." Ray turned right off the highway and we followed a dirt track through the edge of a village to the church. It was locked, of course, and not as pretty up close as it looked from the road. Not worth using film on, film that was now rationed to two photos a day. We turned around and headed back to the highway, but before we could reach it we were stopped by another motorcycle policeman with a large gun on his back. Where did he come from?

"It is not possible to be here."

"We just wanted to look at the church."

"It is not possible to be here."

So much for sightseeing.

The road grew worse as we traveled away from Moscow, and sometimes we passed workers making repairs.

125

These road crews were mostly women, broad and strong, wearing the now familiar house dresses and head scarves. They shoveled asphalt, patted it down, and then leaned on their shovels and brooms while the roller operator—always male—crushed and smoothed it. We saw women working along railroad tracks, shoveling gravel onto the roadbeds and sometimes hefting ties into place. Women dug ditches too. We found it shocking at first, but after a few weeks it became almost normal.

Hedrick Smith reported that eighty-five percent of Soviet women worked in 1974, in all kinds of jobs, but despite socialist doctrine and a constitution that declared equality for women, most women performed low-paying jobs that men didn't want. About seventy percent of doctors were women, but their pay was lower than average. Other specialties that drew women, like teaching, were also near the bottom of the pay scale. And because even male workers earned little, few married women had the option of not working. So it was women who swept the city streets with crude twig brooms, and in deep winter shoveled snow.

Arthur Miller, in his 1969 essay in *In Russia*, beautifully describes such a scene:

"I was sitting on the ground floor of a building belonging to the Writers' Union with five or six Russian writers, when I noticed a gigantic figure just outside the French windows, a person big to begin with but enlarged by a quilted coat and immense felt boots. The conversation within revolved around literature and publishing; outside, this person was digging a ditch in the frozen earth and casting shovelfuls of ice onto a growing pile. Suddenly I realized this was a woman, a woman stabbing a space into that stubborn ground in cold that made it hard to breathe. I said, gesturing toward the window, that it was a pretty cold day to be digging. The others barely glanced at her and went on with the conversation. They did not seem particularly heartless men, and of course most of the people who load snow onto trucks to clear the streets are women. It is even possible that they would defend the use of women for such work on grounds of sexual equality . . . . With the subway gleaming underground and immense modern buildings rising all around us, this woman digging a ditch in such frightfully cold weather while socially conscious writers in a warm room spoke in perfect ease of spiritual matters—one knows at such moments that historic Russia is not yet dead." [22]

Whenever we mentioned we were going to Georgia the Russians would smile and nod and say "Everything's better in Georgia," and "You can buy anything in Georgia—even a submarine!" often rubbing their thumb and middle fingers together in the age-old sign for money. We were looking forward to seeing this magic land where the sun always shines and everything can be had for the asking, but first we had to traverse the Caucasus Mountains, and we still faced miles of rolling steppe. One day we saw oil wells standing tall against pale blue skies. Another day huge piles of coal peaked against the horizon, and along the road we saw men, dirtied from hours underground, walking slowly home from the mines.

The earth was clearly bountiful here in the south, dark and rich. This is where the huge state or collective farms grew wheat and corn, miles and miles of corn grown tall through the summer and now nearing harvest. Despite the increasing availability of fresh food we still struggled; but here was corn on the cob for the taking. On a quiet stretch of road Ray pulled over, yanked open the engine compartment to camouflage his mission, and ducked into the field. A few minutes later he returned with six beautiful cobs of corn. First the toilet paper, now this. Our transition from honest citizens to thieving miscreants was complete.

That night we cooked it, standing over our little gas flame, waiting impatiently, saliva flowing, for that first taste of tender, juicy, buttery corn we knew so well.

It turned out to be field corn, meant for farm animals. It never got tender or juicy, but we ate it anyway. When we later met an Australian couple in Pyatigorsk they confessed they too had stolen corn. But they didn't eat theirs; they threw it away. Wimps.

I have said before that we often got lost. Road signs were essentially nonexistent, especially in the south, so most of the time we just followed our noses. One evening, at the end of a long and frustrating drive, we found ourselves in a sizable town. We had no idea where the campground was. We followed what we thought was the main road, then followed it again when it turned left. Suddenly we were on a muddy, potholed street. Could this be the main road? It could, but maybe we were supposed to go straight? We were lost.

An old man was walking by and Ray insisted I ask him where the campground was. I was tired of being everyone's translator. I was also sure the old man wouldn't know. The more often I asked directions the more I was convinced that people didn't know anything about the towns or roads beyond their own village or street, and to be polite they would just agree with whatever I said.

"Is Rostov in this direction?"

"*Da.*"

"But could it be that road over there?"

"*Da.*"

I said asking was a waste of time; Ray said it wasn't. So we had this journey's first major argument. The result was that I asked, and the man pointed straight down the road. But we were soon lost again.

"It's got to be this way," Ray said.

"No. I'm sure it's this way."

"It can't be."

"Yes, it is." And so we had an even bigger argument. In fact the biggest ever. Which ended with me saying "If you don't like it, get out and walk," and him saying, "Stop the car." Which I did. And he got out and stomped off in the opposite direction.

I started the engine and drove off. By this time poor Jennifer was wailing in the back seat, sure that she was being kidnapped by an angry woman in a foreign country and would never see her daddy again. I kept driving. And then, after a few blocks, I turned around and drove back and picked him up. And eventually we found the campground.

Ray and I almost never argued; we'd never had such a fight and Jennifer had never seen that side of us. It was clear the stresses we felt from long days on the road, too little sleep, an unhealthy diet, and constant wariness, were getting to us. How did the people who lived here deal with it? Did they feel it? Were they immune, complacent, resigned, or always angry? We had no way of knowing. But all of us were feeling the strain.

A man is standing in the Stalin Museum in front of a portrait of Josef Stalin's mother. He shakes his head in grief and sorrow and heaves forth a sigh:

"Ay, ay, ay! Such a lovely lady. It's such a pity that she didn't get that abortion in time!"

PYATIGORSK

SOUTH OF KHARKOV the landscape had turned from mostly flat to gently rolling fields, and by the time we got to Pyatigorsk we were in mountains. After days and miles staring at an essentially unchanging landscape, the idea of driving through mountains excited us all. And these were the famous Caucasus Mountains, dividing Europe from Asia, with Mt. Elbrus, the highest peak in Europe at 18,510 feet (5,642 metres), at their heart.

The Caucasus is a diverse region, linguistically, culturally, and ecologically. The mountains stretch from the Black Sea in the west to the Caspian in the east, touching Russia (Chechnya and North Ossetia), Georgia, Azerbaijan, Armenia, and Dagestan. The region, as I write this in 2013, is in political turmoil, far different from the peaceful, happily-coexisting image it displayed in the '70s. The lifting of the Soviet fist freed the people of the Caucasus region to admit and even glorify their differences. It also freed old antagonisms.

Unfortunately, the natural landscape reflects the cultural. The region is on the list of 34 world biodiversity hotspots—areas determined to be rich in biodiversity that are threatened by humans. There are some 6,400 species of higher plants in the Caucasus, some of which survived the Ice Age. Wildlife includes brown bears, wolves, bison, leopards, and golden eagles. Their protection should concern us all.

Mt. Elbrus, an inactive volcano, is called by many names and like most distinct peaks was thought sacred by the ancient peoples living around it. It is here that Zeus is said to have chained Prometheus after he stole fire from the gods and gave it to early man. Here Zeus sent the eagle to eat Prometheus's liver, and here he was saved from death by Herakles.

The mountain is also one of the "seven summits"—the highest mountains on each continent—and is popular with climbers.

Some of this was known to us in 1977, but not all. To us, heading into the mountains toward Georgia was simply a wonderful change of pace, and a new adventure. But first, we would have two nights in Pyatigorsk. The camping in Pyatigorsk was, says my somewhat acerbic journal entry, "shitty," but the town was the prettiest we had seen, with countless flowers. The name Pyatigorsk means five mountains, and the town sat on a small plateau at the base of those mountains. It was in this campground that we met Betty and Ian, an Australian couple who were following a similar itinerary to ours. They planned to drive through Africa and were traveling in a Range Rover well equipped for the purpose, with jerry cans, winches, a spare wheel, myriad tools, and an ice maker—from which would come our first iced drink in months. We would meet them again as our paths crossed, and we continued corresponding with them for several years after.

Now they confessed they were utterly frustrated with the Soviet Union. They had believed what the glowing brochures told them, and were shocked by what they were actually seeing. They complained bitterly about the quality of service—or lack thereof—and the long waits to buy things. We sympathized, for despite our more realistic expectations, our frustrations ran just as deep.

Pyatigorsk is clearly remembered by all of us for two events. The first was that Ray and I took advantage of the spa, splurging and spending one dollar each on mineral baths. Jennifer stayed with Ian and Betty in the campground while we indulged ourselves. There has been a spa here since 1803, and the building we entered looked as if it must have been the original structure. Old and grandly high ceilinged, it was a vast white-painted cavern staffed by women in white whose voices echoed across the domed spaces.

We were led separately to white-painted cubicles, given large white towels, and told to undress. I was then directed to a second private space with a huge bathtub. The water was running and I climbed in. It was hot and smelled of sulfur. It had been so long since I'd had more than a quick shower in lukewarm or cold water, I could hardly contain my glee. The water ran and ran until I could almost float in it; at last a white-garbed woman walked by, turned it off, ordered me to sit up straight and get my chin out of the water, and left. Fifteen minutes later, alas, she came back and told me my time was up.

I don't think I had ever felt so relaxed. We pulled our heavy limbs into the van, drove back to the campground, pulled out the bed and slept.

It was later that day that Giorgi climbed over the campground wall and approached the van.

"Hello!" he said, "Do you know anyone in Ohio?"

He was a university student studying English, and unlike most students he had a casual, scruffy look about him. He was, we soon learned, disdainful of his country's government and wanted to emigrate if he could. But he wasn't Jewish—the only legitimate way out at the time. He confessed he had had run-ins with the government and said he didn't care anymore what the officials thought; he would do whatever he wanted. I thought his bravado overblown, but he did have very little hope, and no interest in the political system. "They are all corrupt," he said, and we had to agree.

"But I will leave," he said with determination, after we'd talked for several hours. "I won't live my life here." We were sympathetic, but not optimistic. We hoped he wouldn't end in the gulag.

Giorgi was naturally curious about us and America. He knew a good deal from listening to the VOA and BBC, but many of his beliefs were distorted by the fun-house mirror influence of Soviet propaganda. For instance, he asked me if all the women in America wore décolleté clothing. When I pointed out that I wasn't wearing a low-cut shirt he replied that might be because of where I was. I disappointed him by laughing at his naiveté, and saying no.

Giorgi was a fount of information about Pyatigorsk and the Caucasus. It was from him we learned that the writer Lermontov had lived and been killed in a duel here. A monument marked the spot, and a small Lermontov museum honored the writer. As a reader and lover of Russian literature I'm surprised I didn't insist on immediately going there. But more important at that moment was Giorgi's willing promise to take us to the outdoor market the following day. He did, and we spent the morning together, continuing our conversation from the day before. The market was a treat. We bought tomatoes, peppers, watermelon, eggs, onions, pears, and cookies. When we separated for the last time, Giorgi asked if we would send him an English dictionary from the U.S.

"Sure, but can we send you other books as well?

"No, just a dictionary. And you must send it to my friend in Ohio, because the police already know I write to her, and it won't get me in more trouble."

We agreed to do so, and before saying goodbye we traded addresses. It wasn't long after we got back to the U.S. that we got a letter from him, directing us to send things to a friend in Moscow. It was the beginning of a long, involved relationship.

After we left Giorgi at the open-air market we went to a "supermarket," hoping to find some beer. My journal reports that the store was "huge" and I was asked to check my bag. When we got inside, however, we discovered very little on the shelves. There were frozen food freezers, almost all empty, and row upon row of shelves with nothing on them. One shelf held several kinds of canned fish. Seven women worked in the meat department, all bustling away behind glass, but the only things for sale were some cheese and one kind of sausage. At another counter were fancy decorated cakes; we bought a small one, along with some sausage and fruit juice. But as for the beer we'd come for? *Nyet*.

A Georgian went to Moscow to sell his mimosa flowers. Upon his return home his neighbors all came to see him, asking:

"Dear, did you go to the Mausoleum while you were in Moscow?"

"Of course," came the response.

"You saw Lenin?"

"Absolutely," he said.

"Didn't you have to wait in line for a long time? We've heard that you should expect to waste as much as half a day!"

"Ha!" cried the Georgian, "I didn't have to wait at all. I just gave the sentry some money for a bottle of vodka, and he brought the body right out to me."

TBILISI, GEORGIA

FROM PYATIGORSK TO Ordzhonikidze, where, according to my journal, we were supposed to meet "F." It also reports that we called but she was out. Since neither of us can now remember who "F" was, this wouldn't be worth mentioning except that it points up how cautious we had become when talking or writing about the people we met—not because we worried for our safety, but rather we worried for theirs. After Moscow we talked only outside and away from the van about anything that felt risky—people we'd met, experiences we'd had, what we were planning. We had become as paranoid as some of the Russians we met, and though we didn't think the van was bugged, it wouldn't have surprised us. It was only after we left the country that we felt free enough to talk, write and record audio tapes about some of our experiences.

We'd also hidden Tanya's ring. We knew they'd search the car itself, and suspected that when leaving they would also search our luggage. So where to put it? We had some cheap utility candles with us so Ray melted one, added one of Jennifer's red crayons for color, suspended the ring on a piece of string half-way through a cardboard roll from some toilet paper we'd collected, and cast a candle. We then burned it down a half-inch or so and tossed it in the van's only drawer with our silverware and kitchen utensils. And tried to forget it.

Ordzhonikidze was our last stop before heading into the high mountains, and we were excited. It was also our first "motel" stop and we looked forward to real beds. Ray, still suffering from dysentery, was happy to have a real toilet. It was not, however, the way Intourist described it. Or rather, it was a distorted reflection of Intourist's description: shabby bathroom, broken window, doors that didn't properly close, and dreary interiors. The dining room, however, was cheerful, and we had a good dinner. Ian and Betty were also staying; their accommodations sounded worse than ours.

The following day we left early for Tbilisi. Since rain had followed us through much of our trip we weren't surprised to find cloudy skies and rain accompanying us now. But none of that mattered; we were so thrilled to be leaving the endless plains we thought everything was beautiful.

The Caucasus Mountains are steep and rugged, and our road wound up and up through hairpin curves overlooking precipitous drops that lacked railings. A herd of donkeys halted our progress, briefly but charmingly, and in places the road was potholed, rock strewn, muddy, or washed out. A stream flowed downhill on our right through a chasm that narrowed and widened in turn; it must have been a torrent in season. Across it we occasionally spotted villages, some with the same red tiled roofs that are pervasive around the Mediterranean, reminding us how far south we had come.

A church sat alone high on the peak of a steep hill, its dome not onion-like, but simpler, with straight lines and a shallow, inverted bowl for a top. On another hillside white flowers bloomed, but on closer inspection they proved to be not flowers, but sheep. Farther up the road we saw more sheep, and looking beyond them we discovered the shepherd, standing high against the green hillside, leaning on his long staff. His bearded face was half covered by the wide black fur hat that hid his ears and eyebrows. His jacket was heavy and padded, and his black pants were tucked into high rubber boots. Such a picturesque character in the middle of nowhere could not be passed without a photograph.

Ray stopped the car, dug out a package of Camels, and climbed the hill while Jennifer and I sat and watched. The shepherd came partway down to meet him and they talked for a few minutes. Then Ray stepped back, snapped his picture, and came trotting back down the hillside. I could tell he was laughing.

"He wanted to buy my jeans!" he said, climbing into the car.

"Seriously? Way out here?"

"Way out here."

I have to admit we were disappointed. Here was a character who looked like he belonged in a picture book, and all he wanted was to change his look.

Our road continued up and up. Somewhere near the border dividing the Russian and Georgian Republics was a sign in typical, socialist-realism style. On the left, a Russian man dressed in blue overhauls, crisp shirt and blue tie, stood in front of a red building topped by a star. He was shaking hands with a man dressed in traditional Georgian costume: broad fur hat, banded-collar shirt, and a belted black jacket with a knife at his waist. Behind him a view of high mountains. The sign in Russian read: "Inviolable friendship of the peoples of the USSR."

The Soviets were constantly reassuring themselves.

Farther up the road we passed a ruined fort, and pulled off to explore it. There wasn't much left, but a mostly complete and picturesque stone tower made a fine photograph. Farther yet we spotted another small ruin. Since no policeman had stopped us at the fort we pulled off there too. The ruin was a short hike from the road, and there wasn't much left of whatever it had been. It consisted of a rough stone platform with an arch below and a smaller, roofed structure on top. Two short stone pillars supported the roof and were connected by shallow arches to an enclosed space in the rear.

We walked around it, trying to imagine what it looked like new and what it might have been. Ray and I climbed up to sit beneath the front arch so Jennifer could take a photo. The stones were crumbling, and loose slate lay along the top where grass had not yet grown. As we were clambering down Ray spotted some change, a couple of rubles that had no doubt fallen from someone's pocket. He picked it up and we went on our way.

It had taken us seven hours to drive 130 miles, but we reached our destination, another fine motel. This one was better, despite the water in the bathroom sink that never quit running, and the fact that for three days we had to share one set of towels and go without toilet paper. It was definitely better.

And we loved Tbilisi. It's an old city, founded in 479 A.D by a king drawn to the sulfuric hot springs—or so says legend. The city straddles the Kura River, and low hills climb the right bank, surrounding and seeming to protect the old, multi-colored, multi-balconied wooden houses that were surely the most photographed site in Tbilisi. On the opposite side is the contemporary city, with well-built, modern structures that actually had style.

We had three nights there, which wasn't enough. We wished we had planned better and stayed longer. We had the usual quick tour with a guide and then enjoyed exploring on our own. For three days we walked and drove the city and its outlying districts. One afternoon we passed a football stadium where crowds of men were milling in front of a line of blue and white buses. In front of the buses stood a string of policemen, identical in their blue shirts and black pants. They had no weapons that we could see, but it looked like trouble was expected. We turned the car around and left.

Another day we walked the downtown streets and found that it was true, Georgia did have more of everything. The women were well-dressed, slim, and stylish; so were most men, who commonly wore mustaches. They had the dark hair and bronze-tone skin so common around the shores of the Mediterranean.

The shops were clean, well organized, and full of goods waiting to be sold—including shot guns, which surprised us—and there were no lines. Also not present was the double-cashiering system that so plagued shoppers in the north. We found all kinds of food, but especially fruits and vegetables.

The cafes were well organized and uncrowded. It was the closest thing to a western city we saw in the USSR. There was even an automatic car wash. The Georgians were cheerful, friendly, and helpful. And they stared far less—maybe we weren't so obvious here, or maybe they had better things to do.

Walking down a broad, sunny street one afternoon we saw a woman in the traditional widow's garb of black dress and headscarf; beside her was an old, upright scale. We took turns getting weighed, for a few kopeks each. To no one's surprise, we had lost weight. Later, we sat on a park bench and spent an hour visiting with two well-dressed, older, Georgian men. They both spoke English and were surprisingly outspoken and informative. We repeated the usual story of our trip and they told us about the city and its history, even venturing into the politics of the area. It was during this conversation we learned that the small ruin we had stopped at was a shrine, and the money we had taken, an offering. They laughed, but we felt embarrassed and foolish.

The second night of our stay we wanted to eat in the motel dining room, which looked quite pleasant. A sign on the door said they opened at 6 p.m. When we went back at six they were closed but a hand-written note said, "open at 8." At 8 p.m. we returned to find the dining room completely packed, and when we asked to be seated were told we were too late, they had quit serving. So we asked if we could buy a bottle of wine from the bar. No, the bar was closed too, though we could see people sitting inside.

This kind of arbitrariness drove me wild. More than the constant police presence, or the endless drives and schedules that kept us on a tight leash; more, even, than being watched, it was the ability of anyone who had a smidgen of authority to change rules on a whim that pushed all my buttons. Ray, with his even temper, handled it much better than I.

We turned away from the dining room and started upstairs. "If we were at home," I said, burning, "I'd demand to see the manager."

"There's the office," said Ray, pointing to a door on our left. I looked over, saw the sign, and marched back down the stairs. Followed by a wondering Ray and Jennifer, I opened the door and went in.

A young man greeted me. "I wish to speak to the manager," I said in Russian. I must say that nothing improves one's language abilities like anger—not that I'm recommending it. The Russian language flowed flawlessly from my lips throughout this entire encounter. And not only did I speak well, I understood everything.

"One moment." He came back shortly and ushered us into the office of the manager, who greeted us with a friendly smile, and asked what he could do to help. Under normal conditions, this alone would have calmed me.

I explained that we had tried to get into the dining room twice and were turned away, and that we had several times asked to purchase a bottle of wine but were also refused, for no apparent reason. We could see the bar open and people inside. "Why?" I asked. "Why?"

I went into a litany of old complaints, asking why? after each one. My anger carried me, I thought, into silver-tongued eloquence, and I was far more verbose than usual. When I ran out of steam we were gently asked to sit down, the assistant was sent to get us a bottle of wine, and we were offered glasses of wine punch, with a Pepsi for Jennifer.

The manager graciously asked about our trip, how we liked Georgia, where we were going next, why we had come, etc., and we had a very pleasant conversation, though I sulked through the first half of it. The solicitousness of the Georgian manager and his assistant were a far cry from the sullen rudeness we had met with from most Russian officials. An hour later we left bearing our bottle of wine, a pitcher of punch, three Czech beers, and a plate of cookies, and felt like we'd won the lottery. And despite being slightly ashamed of my outburst, I thought we deserved it all.

The next day, our last in the city, we returned to our favorite Tbilisi places, explored some new ones, and treated ourselves to one more loaf of their delicious, heavy bread. Biting down hard Ray felt something, pulled the bread out of his mouth and looked at it, then looked at me.

"Oh, shit," he said. "I've broken a tooth."

Poor Ray had definitely drawn the short straw on this trip when it came to health issues. First diarrhea, now this. And in a country where dental care was poor, and missing teeth were replaced with shiny steel ones. Fortunately, the broken tooth, a molar, wasn't causing pain, but it scared us both. In our typical and predictable pattern, I thought Ray should see a dentist, and he was adamant about not wanting to. We agreed to put it on a "wait-and-see" basis.

Before we left Tbilisi, Ray wrote and mailed a postcard to President Carter, "from the other Georgia." I felt this would surely bring the FBI to our door, but it never did. Maybe presidents get lots of postcards from Tbilisi.

Breshnev is talking to Kosygin:

"The devil only knows what's going on. Everyone's running away! If you were to declare free emigration, perhaps only the two of us would remain here."

Kosygin, avoiding Brezhnev's eyes, muttered:
"Leonid, please—speak only for yourself."

SUKHUMI

OUR DRIVE FROM Tbilisi to Sukhumi was long and hellish. The road was in awful condition, and completely washed out in places. Road-building equipment was parked about but no one was working; there were no detour or safety signs of any kind and we crept through mud and around boulders, frighteningly close to steep drops, before winding our way down the mountains into Sukhumi, on the Black Sea.

The road improved as we left the mountains behind, and we passed several fields growing what looked like small green shrubs. We had never seen tea growing and I was curious. Ray stopped the car, and we walked into a gap between the long rows of low shrubbery. As I was bending over to pick a few leaves to taste, a passing car honked, and we turned to see the passenger waving his index finger at us, then putting his hands to his eyes as if they were binoculars. We quickly climbed back in the van and drove on.

Jennifer had high expectations for the Black Sea, with its promise of swimming and sunbathing, and working off a little energy, and for her sake we wanted that too. And in fact, it was very good. The skies were blue and sunny, the steep and verdant shores were lined with pines and tall cypress trees, and we had plenty of time to visit the beach. Of course we were told we must only enter *here* and turn right and walk down to the foreigner's beach, but we didn't. We entered *here* and turned right, walked about a block and put our towels down in the middle of vacationing Russians.

The beach was crowded, with only a few feet separating one party from another. But "personal space" isn't a problem in a country where families and strangers still share living spaces. The sunbathing Russians, pale escapees from the north, were bright red or, if they had been here awhile, deeply tanned.

One of the benefits of Soviet life were the free or low-cost "spas" dotted all along the coast. Some people were here for their health, others just on vacation. But all were hedonists in the glorious sunshine, and they had no inhibitions about offering their overweight bodies to public scrutiny. On a wooden pier two hefty men, their well-browned bellies hanging over their tight black swimsuits, found a few square feet on a bench to play chess. Large white umbrellas offered spotty shade, and a man wearing shorts and a pile of tall straw hats walked the beach hawking his wares—a rare form of private enterprise.

We too were in bathing suits, which gave us a new kind of freedom. No one could tell we were foreigners and no one stared. It was wonderful! Jennifer and Ray headed for the water and I pulled out a book. But I soon tired of it and turned to people watching before the hot sun drove me to join my family in the water. Refreshed at last, we dressed and headed into town.

Like resort towns the world over, this one had souvenir shops and cafes and sidewalks to stroll upon. It was green, relaxed, and pleasant. Two little girls, about five, in short dresses and with large bows in their hair—a Russian tradition—stood at an outside table eating ice cream with their mother. We decided we too must have ice cream. Later, Ray went to a barber shop for a shave and I teased him about letting a Soviet barber get so close to his throat with a straight razor; he was unfazed.

In Sukhumi, instead of a camping site we had a "bed" which we discovered was a room in a four-plex with bare wood walls, three iron cots, torn curtains and a single light-bulb hanging from the ceiling.

"Well, this is pretty nice," I announced on walking in.

"Yeah, not bad," said Ray. Which proves, if nothing else does, how acculturated we had become.

We had also become inured to the daily requests to sell jeans or anything else we had. Other tourists admitted to selling things, or buying rubles on the black market, and our money was running low. Maybe we should consider it? That thought was on the table when we left our little cabin to go to dinner. Jennifer had been invited by a new friend to have dinner with her family, so Ray and I were on our own.

We walked down to the campground dining room to find it closed. Walking back, we met other campers who recommended a Georgian restaurant just outside the campground fence. "Just go that way," they said, "and you'll find it."

Soon we came upon what looked like a large upside down basket, its four walls made of dark branches woven around heavy wooden stakes. A small sign on the plywood door was the only indication food might be had here. We pushed open the door and walked in.

In the center of a gray concrete floor sat a woman stirring a huge cast iron pot over an open fire. As I walked past she motioned to me to look in and I saw a mound of simmering polenta, a big chunk of melting white cheese in the center. The stirring woman smiled and nodded and said something in Georgian that I accepted as "good!" Above the pot hung racks of meat waiting to be cooked. A single row of rough wooden benches sat around the periphery of the small room, and in front of them were other, higher benches serving as tables.

About half the seating was filled, but we were welcomed warmly, and quickly found a place next to another couple from the campground. Four young Georgian men were our casual waiters, carrying clay pots of wine from table to table, transferring it to clay cups and openly enjoying it themselves. As our wine was being served the woman seated next to us said authoritatively in Georgian, "Bring them meat. And make it good meat!"

Plates of skewered lamb, green salad, and buttery, cheesy polenta soon made their appearance, and we hungrily dove in. It was delicious. And the party was, apparently, just getting started. We conversed with our neighbors, joked with the waiters, drank more wine, ate more lamb and polenta, and had a wonderful, relaxing evening. Walking home we agreed it was by far the best meal we'd had in the Soviet Union.

Maybe it was our earlier decision to think about selling something, or maybe it was the wine or the warm night air, but when Ray left our cabin to retrieve something from the van he didn't immediately turn down the two young women who approached him wanting jeans. Instead, he came and got me.

The four of us retreated to the van, pulled the curtains, and started bargaining. I was still very nervous, but Ray was enthused. Our money was running low; this would help. And for whatever reason, he felt he could trust the buyers. As for them, they wanted all we had—four pair between us—but we firmly said no, only one pair was for sale. In the end they agreed on Ray's best Levis for a price of 80 rubles. They handed over 100 rubles and Ray gave them 20 in change.

And now we had a 100 ruble note ($137) and no re- ceipt to show for it, and we'd never even seen a 100 ruble note and where could we possibly change it? Yikes. I didn't sleep well that night.

The next morning Ray got up early to buy petrol be- fore we got on the road. He arrived at the station at 7 a.m. and sat in a line with others until 9:50 a.m. Then the station operator stepped outside to announce, "Benzine *nyet.*" For- tunately, a young couple he'd been talking to said, "Follow us," and led him across town to an open station that did have fuel—a place he would never have found on his own. We of- ten wondered what would happen if we couldn't find petrol or make it to our next scheduled stay, but we were lucky and we never found out.

From Sukhumi we drove up the coast through Gagra to the little town of Adler on the Russian/Georgian border. It was a short day and an easy drive. We looked around for a place to change the hundred. We wanted a large shop, but nothing here matched that. We could wait. In the meantime we tried to relax by swimming and soaking up the sun.

The next day we continued our drive up the coast to Gelendshik and it was here, in what might pass for a small department store, that we changed the bill. Ray went in and left Jennifer and me waiting outside—in case we had to run for it, I guess. I'm not sure what we expected, but whatever it was never materialized. He bought batteries for our tape recorder, handed over the bill and received his change, no questions asked nor comments made. Whew! And we now had an additional 80 rubles to spend.

Just north of Gelendshik the road turned inland, and we reluctantly waved farewell to the Black Sea with its lush vegetation and warm breezes. Skirting the edge of the Caucasus Mountains, we headed northeast for Rostov-na-Donu, and a campground we'd stayed in on our way south. At least we knew where to find it. From there we retraced our route across the rolling plains and rich earth to Kharkov, where the campground had terrible toilets but a decent restaurant; it was where we first had coffee with a scoop of ice cream. The next morning we turned east for Kiev, the last major city on our USSR itinerary.

A KGB man took notice of an individual whom he met every day. Habitually, in the early morning, despite the cold, this man would tip his hat and say, "Good evening." One time the KGB agent detained the man and asked him, "How come you greet me with 'Good evening' when in fact it's only morning?"

"You'll excuse my saying so," answered the man, "but when I see you, everything goes dark before my eyes."

KIEV, UKRAINE

TRAVEL CAN BE wearying. When you open your mind and heart to new experiences every day, day after day, you feel sated, disinclined to think or move. Your body may trudge on but your mind cannot process all those experiences and will exhaust itself trying.

That's how we felt when we arrived in Kiev, where we were to spend five nights. We were tired of long days on the road, tired of the overbearing police presence, tired of the filthy toilets, tired of constantly being asked for gum, jeans, dollars—anything. And just plain tired. Ray still had dysentery, and I was developing a sore throat. We were looking forward to staying put a few days.

It was here in Kiev, on the Dnieper River, that ancient Rus was founded, and it was here that Vladimir I introduced the religion of the Byzantine Empire to Rus in 988, making Eastern Orthodoxy the state religion and deeply influencing the future country's culture. Kiev's close ties to Novgorod and

Constantinople, and the ancient trade routes that connected them, gave its history a romance that Moscow lacked—at least for me. Kiev's influence faded after the Mongol invasion in 1240. The center of power moved northeast to Muscovy, where it stayed.

In 1977 Kiev had a population of almost two million, but it was an easy city to navigate, and we found the broad streets and abundant greenery a welcome feature. We were now in Ukraine, where the language, though similar to Russian, was different enough that I had to struggle a bit to read and understand. But we found our campground, on the edge of the city, quite easily. It was spacious and not unpleasant, despite the two gates, the guards, and far too many overhead lights that shone all night. A motel was nearby, which was always welcome because we could easily get a meal. There were hot showers, and the squat toilets were regularly cleaned. We were pleased with our decision to spend some time here and quickly settled in. The longer stay would also give Ray a chance to rest, and hopefully recover. We had talked about him seeing a doctor too. And there would be hotels for the collection of much needed TP.

It wasn't long before the KGB—or whoever they were—made their move. Two conservatively dressed young men in their early twenties approached us wanting to talk, and offering to take us on a tour of "their city." We had heard this rote conversation so many times we could have repeated it back to them. We told them we weren't interested.

They were eager though, even happy, to tell us that Elvis Presley had just died. When we asked how they knew this, they cheerfully told us they had seen a copy of *Time* magazine—a dead giveaway that they worked for the government. We told them we had seen Elvis perform in Eugene not long before we left on our trip. That fact, and the recognition that we were saddened by the death of this icon of our youth seemed to inspire them to rhetoric heights. They gleefully lectured us on the evils of Elvis's wealth, his drug use, his flamboyant lifestyle. Such a lifestyle was clearly symptomatic, they said, of America's corrupt society.

From Elvis they turned to Elton John and his supposed ability to buy a new Cadillac every day—abhorrent! Their unfamiliarity with the America we knew was laughable, but the Soviet state was good at indoctrination, and despite anything we could say they knew what was true. Disgusted, we turned away. But not before they insisted on meeting again in a few days. Since we couldn't dissuade them of that idea, we reluctantly agreed.

In Kiev we attended an Orthodox church service. Since the church played an vital role in old Russia we had looked forward to this. It was easy to find St. Vladimir's Cathedral, built in the late 19th century to commemorate the 900th anniversary of the Christianization of Rus by Prince Vladimir. The cathedral is a glorious representation of the Byzantine style. Every wall, niche, and crevice is covered with frescoes by Vasnetsov and other well-known Russian artists, with mosaics by Venetian masters. The seven-domed cathedral barely escaped demolition after the Bolshevik revolution, but was ultimately turned into a museum of religion and atheism.

After World War II the authorities relented and the cathedral was permanently opened, becoming one of the few places tourists, or locals, could attend Russian Orthodox services. The day we chose to attend was St. Mary's day (August 28), and we stood near the entrance as the archbishop and other dignitaries solemnly paraded past us into the church, where candles lit the darkness and reflected off the gold-trimmed icons and frescoes. A choir sang, the priests chanted, and hundreds of people stood transfixed in the huge cathedral, as the chanting and music echoed through the high chamber. (In Orthodox churches there are no pews; everyone stands or mills around, visiting various icons and offering prayers.)

Despite the official atheistic position of the government and the scarcity of open churches, people did attend services. Most were old women, who must have felt they had little to lose. For those with ambitions of any kind, attending church was risky. The relationship between the Communist Party and the church was complex. The Party acknowledged the usefulness of the church, and the Orthodox hierarchy officially supported the state. As Hedrick Smith writes, "Tacitly, the Party has acknowledged Orthodoxy as an essential ingredient in the peculiar mixture of loyalties that holds the Soviet State together, a vital element of its Russianness." [23]

So yes, there were believers, and yes, some of them attended church services. But few people would admit it publicly.

I carried our tape recorder to the service and still have the chants and music I recorded. And I still find it amazing.

There were many tourists in the congregation that day, some of them using their cameras to capture the sights, requiring the use of bright flashes in the candlelit sanctuary. We found this rudeness disheartening and left after 30 minutes. But we went back the next day, when the church was quiet, and we had time and light to more closely and peacefully examine the icons and frescoes.

Throughout the country we had seen locked and neglected churches, some of them beautiful specimens of medieval architecture. One day, south of Moscow, I was waiting in the car while Ray and Jennifer were out taking pictures. We had parked on a deserted street near a large, dilapidated brick church that had once claimed three domes, the central one now completely collapsed. Two onion domes, their wooden ribs nakedly exposed, leaned drunkenly. Weeds sprouted from the rooftop and trees grew through a roofless extension. I watched as an old woman, carrying the ever-present string bag, passed my window along the neglected, broken sidewalk. As she reached the front of the church she paused, and turning toward it she crossed herself, then quickly resumed her walk.

This scene is another of those etched deeply into my memory. I did not share her beliefs, but I felt great sympathy for the loss of her religion. The empty and locked churches moved all of us, not because we felt religion's absence personally, but because so many so obviously did. But as the woman's quick crossing of herself illustrated, the ideas and ideals the old churches represented were so deeply felt that sixty years of enforced atheism could not squelch them.

The Soviet state had denied religion but it could not deny the ideas in people's heads—how they believed or thought or worshipped. Thus it existed as a state atrophied by fear, its ability to innovate or move forward in any direction circumscribed by its own need to keep potentially "dangerous" ideas in check. It had doomed itself from the beginning, with Lenin's muzzling of the newspapers and creation of the Cheka, that instrument of fear and terror. Sixty years is brief in the timeline of history. We felt, even then, that a country that did not trust its own citizens surely could not survive.

Kiev was notable in other ways, for it was here that Ray saw a doctor, and here that we met Sergei, a young man who, he said, converted to Christianity after listening to a recording of the Broadway show, "Jesus Christ Superstar." It happened like this.

About 9:30 one evening we were on our way to the campground after a late dinner. We were driving a broad tree-lined thoroughfare when we noticed that the bus stops along our route held unusually large numbers of waiting people.

"Have the buses stopped running?" I wondered aloud.

"Maybe they're just late," said Ray. Then he said, "Let's be the bus."

At the next stop he pulled the van over and people began climbing in, squeezing themselves onto the bench seat, sitting on laps, and hunching themselves into the space between the back seat and the front, which in our camper van was maybe 18 square feet. We had more people than room.

"Daaaad!" wailed Jennifer, as she scurried over the seat back and found a spot among our sleeping bags.

"It's OK, Jennifer," he said, "they'll be getting out soon." And they did. As we drove the main street our passengers would call out their stops and Ray would pull over and let one or two out. This involved much shuffling of people and belongings but everyone was in a good mood, laughing and commenting on their good luck and the story they would tell when they got home.

But one young couple—Sasha and Tanya—remained. Sasha had a little bottle of Russian cognac with him and offered Ray a drink. Tanya was carrying bundles from her day's shopping, and insisted I take a couple of pears and a twist of newsprint. I opened it to find a few tablespoons of coarsely-ground black pepper, obviously a precious commodity. I tried to give it back but she refused to accept it.

Sasha was not drunk but he'd had enough to feel immune to danger and he was thoroughly enjoying himself. He "loved Americans" and he wanted to talk. Tanya was quite nervous, afraid of being seen by the police, so Jennifer helped them close the van's side curtains and returned to her spot behind the seat. We continued through town. Sasha had a brother who spoke English; he insisted we go and pick him up. It was impossible to say no to happy-go-lucky, cheerfully tipsy Sasha, and we soon found ourselves outside a multistory apartment building. He directed Ray to park in back.

"Lights! Lights!" he yelled as we drove up the alley. He put his hands to his eyes like binoculars and Ray quickly doused our headlights.

"Wait here," he said, climbing out of the car. Tanya stayed with us, and while we waited the two of us struggled through a meaningless discussion about nothing in particular. After a wait that felt dangerously long, her husband returned with his brother, a university student named Sergei.

Sergei was adamant that we couldn't park there any longer; it was too risky. So he squeezed in with Sasha and Tanya and we left—very quietly. Ray slowly backed the van from behind the building, our lights out and our voices silent. Thirty minutes later, after making arrangements to meet Sergei at 10 a.m. the next day, we dropped our passengers a few blocks from their home and headed back to the campground, elated by our little adventure, and hoping our new friends wouldn't regret theirs.

The fear they felt was real, but it wasn't new to them. I have already said that prolonged contact with foreigners was discouraged, perhaps illegal. But people did it anyway, just as they did other law-bending things: because that was how they lived. The threat of the police, maybe even the KGB, was a constant. It was their normal. And it had become ours too.

Ray later confessed that had he been ordered by a policeman to stop that evening—they were generally on foot and held out batons to signal a halt—he would have kept driving until he could drop our passengers someplace safe. I had no trouble imagining us all arrested. Jennifer, instead of going to college, would live out her life cutting firewood in the gulag.

The next morning we went to the zoo and were very sorry we had done so. It was a desperately sad place of tiny cages and pacing, unhappy animals. Sergei had not yet appeared and we patiently patrolled the appointed spot, wondering if he would show and hoping he had not run into trouble on our account. Just as we were about to give up, there he was.

It turned out that Sergei's mother was a doctor, the head of a clinic. When we learned this, Ray immediately asked if he could arrange to see her.

"Of course!" But first we must go to Sergei's apartment and he would call her. I hoped his generosity of spirit wasn't misplaced and that his mother would agree to an appointment before we left Kiev.

The apartment, in an older building near the center of town, was quite nice. We sat down with Sergei and had a rambling two-hour conversation, answering the questions we had answered so many times before, and asking our own, with time out for tea. He admitted listening to the outlawed BBC and VOA and declared he didn't like the way things were. But unlike Georgi, Sergei still had hope. He believed that when "younger people" had the chance to be in government, things would change. He also warned us about the KGB officers in the campground; we said we'd already met.

Sergei proudly showed us the American and English record albums friends in Yugoslavia had sent him. It was then he told us he was a believer, and had become one by listening to the album, "Jesus Christ Superstar." Although his sudden conversion by rock opera was humorous, on consideration it wasn't hard to believe. With so little exposure to Christianity, or any religion, and with only atheistic communism to fill one's natural yearning to know and understand life, I could understand being inspired by those words and that music.

"If my belief is discovered by members of my faculty," he told us, "they could have me removed from the university." He attended church services anyway.

He asked—of course—if we would send him jeans and tapes from home and we agreed. Then he insisted that we accept the gift of a small and lovely old icon. I wanted to say yes because I love icons, but we refused, explaining that it was highly illegal for us to take them out of the country. We also felt they were part of Russia's heritage and should remain there.

"Then you must have this," he said, pulling a large, electric (220 volts) samovar off the dining room sideboard. Again we insisted we could not take such a thing, and what would his parents say? He refused to take no for an answer, said they could easily get another, and that we must take it. His persistence was unassailable and we walked out the door carrying a silver-colored samovar covered with a coat, like a sick baby. It was about 20 inches high and 8–10 inches in diameter. Thinking about how we were going to fit this unbendable object into the van's minimalist storage area almost made my head explode, but Sergei was happy.

He had done as he promised and called his mother, and she agreed to examine Ray. Sergei sat in the back with the side curtains drawn as we drove to the clinic and parked across the street.

"Wait here," he said, and ran inside.

We waited. About 15 minutes later he emerged from the building followed by a woman in her 50s. We watched as they crossed the street and approached the van, then Sergei introduced his mother and we all shook hands. She turned to Ray.

"I understand you are having diarrhea." she said in English.

"Yes," said Ray, "for several weeks."

"I can examine you here," she said.

"In the car?"

"Yes, here. I cannot take you inside. Please lay down on the back seat so I can examine you."

At this Sergei, Jennifer, and I moved away from the van to give them some privacy. Jennifer rolled her eyes at me, as if to say "this is too weird." I had to agree. I turned slightly so I could see, and there was Ray, having his now bare tummy kneaded by the doctor, on her knees in the van, her stethoscope pressed to his belly.

After her examination and some discussion with him about his symptoms she said she had medicine that would help. She and Sergei returned to the clinic and the three of us climbed back in the car, hardly daring to laugh at what had just taken place.

At last Sergei returned with two kinds of pills and strict instructions on how to take them. He then took us to an outdoor market where he left us to go to the university. We promised to write and send what he'd asked for; then we climbed back in the van and drove to the campground.

We groaned in unison when we saw the KGB duo waiting at our campsite.

"I'm not talking to them," I said. "Tell them I'm sick," and I ran off to the toilets leaving my husband to do the dirty work. My journal reports that "Ray told them I had a sore throat and that we were too tired to talk. They left rather unhappily and we didn't see them again."

The next day—our last in Kiev—was an easy one. We did more sightseeing, strolled in the riverside park, ate in a local restaurant, and treated ourselves to yet more ice cream. Our journey was coming to an end and we were all happy about it. We had only two more stops before the Romanian border, and I for one couldn't wait.

The official population census. An official asks, "How old are you, Grandpa?"

"Twenty-one."

"What!" exclaimed the shocked census-taker. "You're already deep into old age!"

"That's right. But if you'll excuse my saying so, I can't call the past sixty years 'living.'"

VINNITSA, CHERNOVTSY
AND THE BORDER

VINNITSA, 159 MILES (256k) west of Kiev, was notable
for being the site of one of Hitler's bunkers, and after we got
settled in the campground we drove a few miles out of town
to see it. There wasn't much, a few giant chunks of concrete.
But during the war the site, called Wehrwolf, had been extensive, with its own water and power supply, an airfield, a
swimming pool, and three underground bunkers, the largest
with walls 8 feet (2.5 m) thick. Built in 1941–42 by POWs
and slave laborers, who were afterward killed to protect the
secret location, it was visited by Hitler just three times. In
March 1944 the retreating Germans blew up the site. The
giant blocks of concrete are the only visible remains.

After one night in Vinnitsa we drove to Chernovtsy,
where we were booked into a "first class" hotel. We had anticipated a pleasant last night in the country but it turned out
to be a pretty crummy place. It did have hot water, so we

again used the bathtub to wash clothes, which we hung on the balcony to dry before going out to eat. On our return we were told—in no uncertain terms—that the laundry must be taken down immediately; the hotel could not permit its beauty to be sullied in such a manner. And though we found this description of the hotel humorous, we did as we were told.

The next day we drove to the border.

It's impossible to describe how we felt on leaving this country we had so longed to see. Relief, almost giddiness, predominated. Now we would be free of the overbearing state presence that permeated everything and put an unwelcome weight on our shoulders. We would be free of driving restrictions, free of fear, free of the staring, and free of being constantly asked for goods or dollars.

We felt anxious about the search that would surely take place, and the questions that might be asked. We had Tanya's diamond ring after all; Ray had souvenir rubles tucked into his shoe; we didn't have receipts for every item we'd purchased during our long stay. And who knew what other obstacles they might arbitrarily put in our path?

We felt sadness too, for the people we were leaving behind, for their trapped lives and lost dreams, and for the ideas that would die within them. I thought about the guide in Vinnitsa who, just two days earlier, had told us his lifelong dream was to visit America. We had heard so many dreams like this that would surely be thwarted; how could we not feel sad?

There was anger as well, against the injustices that plagued ordinary citizens every day, against the corrupt leaders who refused to see clearly, and against those in the west who couldn't see past the false bluster that poured from the Kremlin daily.

We had been discouraged by the sullenness and the lack of care or responsibility that we saw everywhere, but we were shocked by the awful roads, the shoddy construction that began decaying before it was finished, the lack of proper plumbing outside the cities, the country's inability to feed itself, and by the censorship and even imprisonment of their own best writers and artists, the ones who dared to show the way. Could this really be the powerful enemy that so frightened Americans? Yes, they had the hardware, the missiles, the nuclear bombs. Even so, it seemed impossible. The Soviet Union was a country drowning in a quicksand of corrupted ideals and false visions. We knew it had to end, but we would have vehemently denied it could happen just twelve years hence.

We drove to the border station and parked. There were no cars ahead of us on this morning. It was a smaller station than the one we had passed through in the north but it still had its brown-clad soldiers and abundant guns. We were ordered to get out of the van and remove our bags and belongings. When everything was piled outside they began their search of the automobile itself. Just as in the north they fed long wires into every crevice and hole. They peered into cupboards but removed nothing. One soldier opened the only drawer and picked up the partially burned candle that hid Tanya's ring. He held it up, turned it slightly in the light, and tossed it back in the drawer. I thought I was going to faint.

Another soldier was looking through our papers and held up a single sheet of writing he'd pulled from under the rear passenger seat. I recognized it as notes I had made, lost, and given up finding.

"Oh," I said, reaching for it, "I've been looking for that." He quickly—and rather smugly—jerked it high and away from me and handed it to another soldier. I shrugged, it was nothing important. (Our journals, fortunately, were in our duffle bags, which they never opened.)

Soon a box of audio cassettes was upended onto the van floor. A guard shuffled through them and picked one.

"Play this!" he ordered. Oh shit, I thought, for we had stupidly made recordings during our visit that we planned to send my parents once out of the country. They described—and often vilified—what we were seeing. Some were recorded over music we had brought, others were on new cassettes; all had handwritten labels. I had no idea what we'd hear when I pushed the button.

". . . and the Colorado rocky mountain high; I've seen it rainin' fire in the sky . . ."

John Denver's distinctive voice soared over the hum of the search and across the tarmac, and my knees wobbled for the second time that morning.

Meanwhile, on the other side of the car, Ray was having his own problems.

"Prepare your instruments!" said the uniformed woman.

"What?"

"Prepare your instruments; your, uh, tools. They wish you to remove the door panels."

"*Nyet!*" said Ray.

"You must!" said the woman.

"No." said Ray loudly. "We are tourists! We've signed

your pledge saying we have no Bibles, no guns, no illegal currency. "

Ho, I thought, what about those rubles in your shoe? But I could tell he was angry and on a roll, and I was proud of him.

"We came to visit your country and you make us feel like prisoners! We are not criminals, we are tourists! You have no right to do this."

Bravo! I thought again of the French woman on the Finnish border and hoped this would be another case of them backing down in the face of adamant refusal. We had been warned by other tourists in the campgrounds, some of whom visited the country frequently, that we must never let the border guards start taking the car apart, because they wouldn't stop. And they wouldn't put it back together either. Ray stood his ground and the searchers moved on to something else without comment. Eventually I turned off John Denver, the soldiers told us to reload our baggage, and our passports were returned. We had been there about 90 minutes.

A month later, in Italy, we picked up a letter from Ian and Betty, the Australians we had met in Pyatigorsk. Crossing that same Ukraine-Romania border a few days behind us, their journals had been discovered and they were accused of writing lies.

"There are no lines for food in the Soviet Union!" claimed the interrogator. The offending pages were ripped out, their belongings intensively searched, and they were held at the border and questioned for 24 hours. We considered ourselves very lucky.

We crossed into Romania with some trepidation. It was, after all, a Communist country. We expected a similar welcome. We drove some distance before coming to the border crossing, a much smaller station than the one we had just left. One or two other cars were ahead of us. We first had to drive through a basin filled with a smelly chemical, then the entire car was sprayed. At last we were allowed to proceed, coming to rest under a small overhang. When we opened the car doors a powerful chemical smell engulfed us, and fumes burned our eyes. We never learned what it was.

These border guards, unlike their neighbors, were cheerful and even laughing. We laughed with them. There was a brief, cursory search. Our passports were carried inside and we prepared for a long wait, but within ten minutes they were back, and after we changed money we were on our way.

It felt wonderful! Now we were free to go anywhere we liked, and to choose any road at any time. Now we could spend the night wherever we wished. Now we could stop and walk through a village, inspect a church, follow a trail.

Nicolae Ceausescu was the country's leader in 1977, but he was not yet the tyrant he would become. We knew Romania had closer ties to China than to the Soviet Union, but we didn't know what that meant for the population, or for us. It was with great relief that we found far more food, more goods of all kinds, and better roads. And in the first shop we visited we found toilet paper—from China. You know you've been down when the sight of toilet paper, in clear plastic wrapping covered with red Chinese writing, makes you feel ecstatic.

The landscape had grown hillier after we turned south in Vinnitsa, and now we found ourselves in gently curving mountains covered with green grass and evergreens. We were in old Moldavia, and we turned the car toward Sucivita and Moldavita to see the famous painted monasteries. We were all feeling strangely lifted and content. I felt as though I could almost float. Jennifer said, "Dad, can you stop the car?"

"Sure, why?"

"I want to run for awhile."

He pulled the car over and she climbed down and took off down the hill in front of us. There was no traffic, and it was a beautiful, sunny morning. We followed her slowly, not talking. After some time I said, "Strange, she's never wanted to do this before."

"It's a release from the pressure," said Ray.

"Yeah," I agreed. "There she goes; freedom in tennis shoes."

A Soviet athlete had just won the gold medal in the Olympic Games for the hammer-throw. Photographers and reporters surrounded him and asked: "Say, how did you manage to throw the hammer such an incredibly long distance?"

"That was nothing," said the athlete. "Had they also given me the sickle, I'd have thrown it twice as far!"

BEYOND THE SOVIET UNION

THAT NIGHT WE camped in a little pull-out beside the road, surrounded by trees and greenery, overlooking rolling hills. There was little to no traffic. We had been able to easily purchase canned goods and even a pre-made salad that looked delicious—no lines, no double-cashier system, and plenty to choose from. It had been a good day, and we were looking forward to relaxing and celebrating our newfound freedom. We hadn't seen a single policeman since leaving the border and no one arrived on a motorcycle to say stopping here was "not possible."

Ray and I were having a glass of wine when a woman in peasant dress approached the van. We were sadly deficient in languages but we did have a Romanian dictionary and phrase book so we greeted her in her native language. It was clear though, that we couldn't go much further. We offered a glass of wine and she accepted, and we sat amiably together while she chatted away.

After so many years of travel it still surprises me when people who know you don't understand a word they are saying continue to speak as though you do. It has happened so frequently I assume I'm missing a gene. Unlike them, I find it impossible to talk back when it's clear I won't be understood. Instead, I nod dumbly and try to escape.

But on this calm and quiet evening we weren't escaping anything, we were happy to be where we were. Using our dictionary we asked if it was all right to spend the night here and she said yes, but the horses might wake us in the morning. That sounded more like fun than a problem. She talked on, sometimes waving her arm and urging us to do something, but we had no idea what. As she was finishing her second glass of wine a boy appeared at our open door—her son, who was about six. The woman left shortly after but he stayed, so we fixed our dinner and shared it with him, Jennifer reluctantly giving up the last of her new-found lemonade.

We had finished eating, and I was beginning to wonder what to do with the boy, when a girl a little older than Jennifer appeared, to be followed shortly by a woman who was surely grandma, followed by the original visitor herself. We were becoming quite a party. They began doing a kind of pantomime, all saying the same thing over and over and pointing down the hill.

"I think they want us to move the van," said Ray.

"Where?"

"How do I know?"

"But I like it here."

"So do I. But I think we should move."

So we stowed our belongings and the four of them piled in the car. Following their waving arms and unknown words we headed down the hill: go a quarter-mile, turn right, go across a field and stop right here, in front of the little white plastered house. The van was pitched forward at an alarming angle, but if that was where they wanted us, there we would stay.

We were immediately invited inside. The house consisted of a single room with a barn attached to the back. A thin old man, grandpa, greeted us on entry. Ray returned to the van for a pack of Camels, and grandpa promptly lit up. My journal describes the room, which I estimated to be 12 x 15 feet. It contained two double beds, a chest, a table, and a wood stove holding a cheerful little fire. On one bed a baby was sleeping. The brown plaster walls had no decorations save for a small portable radio hanging on a nail. There was one small window. I saw no sink or running water, and only a single kerosene lamp. It seemed impossible that all of them lived here, but there was no other, obvious, answer.

We were each handed a cup of warm milk and we made what conversation we could. I tried Russian on them but got nowhere. Our dictionary was in the car, but playing charades can get you a long way, so we left it there. After we handed back our empty cups the woman went to the radio and switched it on. A strident male voice broke through the companionable silence and she frowned and shook her head and turned the dial; gypsy music filled the room.

She motioned me to join her. Her daughter grabbed Jennifer's hand, grandma stood up and very quickly the five of us were circling the room, clapping to the rhythm of the violins and sending smiles across the floor. We had worked our way through two tunes before a young man entered, giving us an excuse to bring our visit to a close. We said goodnight and returned to the van, wondering how we could possibly sleep at such an angle. Starting the engine, however, would surely have caused concern inside the house. We stayed put.

But we didn't sleep much. Jennifer, in her hammock, managed better than Ray and I. We alternated between sliding downhill and tugging ourselves back to the top of the bed. Thankfully the sun did rise, and we piled out of the van early, knowing the family would surely be up. The daughter led Jennifer to the barn at the rear of the house, where she handed her a cup of fresh milk and encouraged her to milk one of their four cows. But, as our daughter reported in her journal, "it didn't work."

As we prepared to leave, everyone gathered in front of the house and Ray took photos. (We had managed to purchase a few spare rolls of film from a fellow camper.)

A neighbor woman appeared from over the hill and seeing the camera, hurriedly replaced her patterned headscarf with a borrowed black one, then smiled for her photo. We gave them what gifts we could rummage from our belongings, cigarettes, tea, and a few other small items. The girl had been admiring a silver ring I wore so I gave it to her, and was rewarded with a beautiful smile and energetic little twirl.

Unlike the Russians, these Romanians were huggers, so everyone got a hug in turn and sometimes two. At last we were able to depart, retracing our path across the field, waving goodbye until they were out of sight, and making our way slowly back to the highway.

These photographs and addresses, and others from the Soviet Union, were lost when a bag was stolen from our van in Rome. Of course we felt awful that people who expected to hear from us never would, but save reversing course there was nothing we could do. It was not our fault, but I felt guilty nonetheless.

We didn't spend much time in Romania, though we loved the mountains and the green, rolling hillsides. We went to Brasov and Poiana Brasov, visited "Dracula's castle," and spent a couple of nights in Bucharest. It was a rural and generally impoverished country where ox-drawn carts were common and most labor was done by hand. We watched women transferring corn from a full oxcart into a waiting boxcar, tossing the ears up and in, one by one by one.

It was our visit to the International Hotel in Bucharest that brought home to us how deeply removed we had been from western society. Where did this sparkling lobby, with modern fixtures and shining floors, come from? And look at that clean dining room, with bountiful food and—smiling service? My word! The words culture shock couldn't encompass all that we felt. It was like stepping into an alternate universe.

After visiting the gift shop, where we splurged on a small handwoven rug and an embroidered blouse for our daughter, we headed for the border. We had promised Jennifer at least a week on the Adriatic coast and were all anxious to get there.

We crossed the Danube River and drove headlong into Yugoslavia's spectacular mountains, and our third Communist country. If Romania had been a step up in freedom and goods, Yugoslavia was yet another. In many ways we felt we were already back in the west. Western magazines and newspapers appeared, and we bought our first European edition of *Newsweek*. Food was plentiful, some of it even familiar, and we were eating better and doing more of our own cooking. Soon we would start to regain the pounds we had lost.

The poverty we saw on entering the country eased as we traveled westward toward the coast. We spent a few days in lovely Sarajevo, a city that offered enticing insights into multiple cultures. We admired the minarets and bargained happily in the markets, convinced that here people had made peace with their differences. But just as the Caucasus region was torn by suspicion and war when the Soviets withdrew, so too was Yugoslavia after Marshall Tito's death in 1980. The city that we loved for its diversity would too soon be ripped asunder.

From Sarajevo to Mostar, through yet more mountains with steep drops and distant views. We found ourselves relaxing at last, the anxiety of our weeks in the Soviet Union fading in the face of the awesome scenery and peaceful towns.

From Mostar to Dubrovnik to Split, and a week camping on the coast, where the water was as clear and green as liquid glass. We walked the rocky beaches, drank wine, ate well, waded in the sea—it was too cold now to swim—and slept well. I felt as though life was returning after a long siege of illness, and for Ray that was actually true—the pills had worked and his diarrhea was gone. Heading north we visited the caves at Podornja, where white, blind lizards—with such human-like skin and "hands" they made my skin crawl—lived deep underground. Then north again to see the Lipizzan stallions at Lipica, in what is now Slovenia. And from there we turned west toward Italy, and home.

★

We had started our long journey visiting American friends in Frankfurt, Germany, and we returned there for three weeks while our van made its way across the Atlantic to New Jersey. The owner of the apartment, Thelma, was a long-time friend of my mother, and her daughter Sue was my old friend. Thelma taught school on the U.S. military base at Frankfurt. She was a delightful woman, energetic and positive, but also opinionated, and she never hesitated to speak or act on her beliefs. Her conservative outbursts could drive me to distraction and we argued occasionally, but always as friends. Thelma and Sue had both visited the Soviet Union with a tour group several years earlier. I knew Thelma—a fervid anti-Communist—would be anxious to hear our thoughts. She turned first to our daughter.

"Well, Jennifer," she said enthusiastically. "Tell me what you learned on your trip—no, tell me what you learned in the Soviet Union."

Jennifer paused a moment. Thelma was a teacher after all, consideration was due. She said, "I learned the difference between free and not free."

"Ha!" said Thelma. "Good for you!"

Jennifer had learned her lesson well. Indeed, even the most inattentive traveler—and she wasn't—couldn't fail to mark freedom's absence. Yet the difference between "free and not free" was not as black and white as the lines on a map or our cultural dispositions suggested. Our experience in the Soviet Union revealed a more nuanced understanding: freedom can be a muddy shade of gray.

Today we are far removed from 1977. Complexity has increased exponentially. The changes—economically, technologically, politically—are vast. Yet freedom—whether you think of it as self determination, liberty, independence or something else—remains a touchstone for all of us. Freedom, even when it's a muddy shade of gray, is humanity's most precious entitlement. In remembering the years when it was lost to so many, we help to keep it alive for all.

AFTERWORD

RETURNING HOME AFTER our seven-month absence (including a month driving across the U.S.) was a shock. For weeks I felt as though a thick screen of Plexiglas® stood between me and everyone I talked to. As is usual with such a trip, we felt we'd been gone for years while those at home expressed wonder that we were back so soon. And while many were curious about the USSR portion of our journey, few showed more than a passing interest in the rest of it.

But the trip instilled in all of us a confidence we would never otherwise have found. We had, through 17 countries, languages, and cultures, stretched our minds and psyches to handle situations never previously encountered. Each day on the road had tested us, and we had, we thought, aced the tests.

I returned to the university and my classes, but the need to work full time quickly overcame my need to graduate. I did, however, stay involved with the department in other ways. And I started freelancing for the local weekly newspaper. Ray returned to his job with Southern Pacific, and Jennifer went back to school. Her European experiences would eventually lead her to become an environmental anthropologist.

Tanya's ring was safely returned. We did sell the van, and it did, as planned, cover a big chunk of our expenses.

Of the people we met we remained in touch only with Giorgi, who for many years was a regular correspondent through his contact in Moscow. We sent him jeans and other items he could sell for money to emigrate.

A few years later we learned that his friend in the American Embassy had been illegally allowing packages such as ours to travel through diplomatic mail; that discovery led to an "international incident." She was sent home and we temporarily lost contact with Giorgi. Sometime in the mid '80s he turned up in San Francisco, conveniently married to a woman who had helped him reach America—he had said he would leave the Soviet Union and he had. We continued to hear from him sporadically, and in the early '90s, when we were living in Portland, he came to visit. He was an aspiring film maker then, but making little headway. At some point he returned to Russia and we lost track of him.

Because we lived in a democratic republic, my idea didn't, like Ilya's, die. The epiphany I had sitting on my kitchen floor had led me inexorably to Russia and then to the idea of traveling there. And because I didn't reject that idea or discard it for being unworkable, I was ultimately able to persuade my family that we could take that six-month journey. My idea became theirs, and with their help, commitment, and passion, it coalesced into reality.

The trip that was meant to "get travel out of my system" instead inspired an itch for more in all of us. With only average incomes we managed to take a three-month trip in 1981, a six month trip in 1987, and to spend a year living in Turkey in 1997–98. During that year our savings grew, thanks to an irrationally exuberant stock market, so instead of being financially prudent and immediately finding jobs on our return, Ray and I enjoyed a four-month journey by car across the length and breadth of Mexico in 1998, and a three-month trip in 1999 across the U.S. on highway 20, from Newport, Oregon to Boston, Massachusetts, and on to Nova Scotia. And then we went back to work. And in 2000 we bought a tiny house in a tiny French village that we utterly loved for six short years.

Throughout our travels many people have asked how we managed all this. There isn't one simple answer. But when some said enviously, "Oh, I wish I could do that!" we always replied, "You can. You just have to choose."

ENDNOTES

1. All the jokes leading the chapters are from *Forbidden Laughter (Soviet Underground Jokes)*, compiled and edited and carried across the border in a false-bottom box known as a "skull" by Emil Draitser, illustrated by Igor, and translated by Jon Pariser. (Almanac Publishing House, Los Angeles, 1978).

2. *Samizdat* is the name given to underground writings that were passed secretly from person to person. These could be anything from short stories or poems to political writings or cartoons. *The Chronicle of Current Events* was the most organized and best known of such publications. Sixty-four issues focusing on human rights were published between 1968 and 1983. The anonymity of authors was protected, and regular sections were dedicated to arrests, searches, interrogations, in prisons and camps, and persecution of various ethnic groups and religions. Copies were regularly smuggled to the West. Some editions can be viewed on the website of Amnesty International.

3. Intourist was the official Soviet state travel office, in charge of the majority of travel by foreigners to and within the country. It was founded in 1929 by Joseph Stalin and was staffed by NKVD and later KGB officials. Intourist has been privatized since 1992.

4. On the official exchange one ruble was worth $1.37 in 1977. On the black market you could sometimes get four rubles to the dollar.

5. No credit cards were accepted in the Soviet Union, nor were there any charge accounts or checks. Everything was paid in cash.

6. Grigory Potemkin, a minister to Catherine II (the Great), is said to have erected prosperous-looking fake settlements along the banks of the Dnieper River to fool the Empress. Many historians now view this tale as a myth—or at best, a misunderstanding of the actual

occurrence. The phrase "Potemkin's village" has, however, made its way into common usage.

7. Felber, John E., *American's Tourist Manual for the U.S.S.R*, (International Intertrade Index, Newark, NJ, 1976).

8. Massie, Suzanne, *Land of the Firebird: The Beauty of Old Russia* (Simon and Schuster, 1980), p. 374.

9. Massie, Robert K., *Peter the Great: His Life and World*, (Alfred A. Knopf, 1980), p. 365.

10. *Ibid.*, p. 366

11. Smith, Hedrick, *The Russians*, (Ballentine Books, New York, 1976), paperback, p. 174.

12. We had been told before we left the U.S. that Soviet maps were all "deliberately wrong," but we bought a book of maps anyway, in Leningrad. However, on using it we discovered that it was indeed "wrong." Distances were incorrect, rivers might be on the wrong side, landmarks in the wrong place, etc. It was basically useless and added to our frustration.

13. We had brought photographs of our home and family, along with other places of interest. One was a picture taken at Fort Ross, a Russian settlement (1812 to 1841) on the California coast. Every Russian we showed that photo to, including Marina, the history major, was shocked. A few refused to believe the Russians had ever been in California.

14. Thompson, M.W., *Novgorod the Great: Excavations at the Medieval City Directed by A. V. Artsikhofsky and B.A. Kolchin*, (Praeger, 1967).

15. Gail Lenhoff and Janet Martin, "Marfa Boretskaia, Posadnitsa of Novgorod: A Reconsideration of Her Legend and Her Life." *Slavic Review* 59, no. 2 (2000): 343–68.

16. We were told then that about 20,000 Americans visited the Soviet Union annually. I've been unable to find any statistics, so this may or may not be accurate.

17. Smith, Hedrick, *The Russians,* (Ballentine Books, New York, 1976) paperback, p. 226.

18. Bukovsky, Vladimir, *To Build a Castle: My Life as a Dissenter,* translated by Michael Scammell, (Viking Press, New York, 1979). p. 123

19. Trading small pins (*znachki*) that identified cities, towns, and events was a popular hobby with Russians and tourists alike.

20. From an article by A. Yemelyanov in "Problems of Economics," March 1975, pp. 22–34: cited in *The Russians,* by Hedrick Smith, p. 266.

21. Bukovsky,Vladimir, *To Build a Castle: My Life as a Dissenter,* p. 141.

22. Miller, Arthur, and Inge Morath, *In Russia,* (Viking Press, New York, 1969), p. 15.

23. Smith, Hedrick, *The Russians,* (Ballentine Books, New York, 1976) paperback, p. 583.

SELECTED BIBLIOGRAPHY

This list includes most books referenced in the text and others that I found useful. Readers wishing to know more about Russia and the U.S.S.R will find these a good beginning. Though some are out of print, used copies can still be found.

Amalrik, Andrei, *Will the Soviet Union Survive Until 1984?* (Harper & Row, New York, 1970).

Bukovsky, Vladimir, *To Build a Castle: My Life as a Dissenter,* translated by Michael Scammell (Viking Press, New York, 1979).

Draitser, Emil, *Forbidden Laughter (Soviet Underground Jokes),* (Almanac Publishing House, Los Angeles, 1978).

Hosking, Geoffrey, *Russian History: A Very Short Introduction* (Oxford University Press, 2012).

Kollontai, Alexandra, *The Autobiography of a Sexually Emancipated Communist Woman* (Prism Key Press, New York, 2011).

Labedz, Leopold & Max Hayward, editors, *On Trial: The Case of Sinyavsky (Tertz) and Daniel (Arzhak),* (Collins and Harvill Press 1967).

Lovell, Stephen, *The Soviet Union: A Very Short Introduction* (Oxford University Press, 2009).

Massie, Suzanne, *Land of the Firebird: The Beauty of Old Russia* (Simon and Schuster, 1980).

Massie, Robert K., *Peter the Great: His Life and World* (Alfred A. Knopf, 1980).

Massie, Robert K., *Nicholas & Alexandra: The Fall of the Romanov Dynasty* (Modern Library Edition, an imprint of Random House, 2012).

Miller, Arthur, and Inge Morath, *In Russia* (Viking Press, New York, 1969).

Pond, Elizabeth, *From the Yaroslavsky Station* (Universe Books, 1984).

Reed, John, *Ten Days That Shook the World* (Penguin Classics 2007).

Smith, Hedrick, *The Russians* (Ballentine Books, New York, 1976).

Solzhenitsyn, Aleksandr I. *The Gulag Archipelago, 1918–1956: An Experiment in Literary Investigation I-II*, translated from the Russian by Thomas P. Whitney. (Harper & Row, New York, 1973).

Solzhenitsyn, Aleksandr I. *One Day in the Life of Ivan Denisovich*, translated by Ralph Parker (E.P. Dutton & Co., 1963).

Voinovich, Vladimir, *The Ivankiad: Or the Tale of the Writer Voinovich's Installation in His New Apartment* translated by David Lapeza (Farrar, Straus and Giroux, New York, 1976).

Voznesensky, Andrei, *Nostalgia for the Present,* Vera Dunham and Max Haward editors. (Doubleday 1978).

Karen Gilden is a long-time freelance writer and editor, whose articles have appeared in both local and national publications. She is the author of *Tea & Bee's Milk: Our Year in a Turkish Village* (2008) and *How to Plan Your Trip to Europe* (1995). Learn more at **karengilden.com**

5007203R00131

Printed in Germany
by Amazon Distribution
GmbH, Leipzig